T0105662

A TEXAS TALE
OF THE
DEPRESSION

A TEXAS TALE
OF THE
DEPRESSION

WANDA HARRIS ARNOLD
Presented by Suzanne Arnold Kelley

authorHOUSE®

AuthorHouse™
1663 Liberty Drive
Bloomington, IN 47403
www.authorhouse.com
Phone: 1 (800) 839-8640

Published by AuthorHouse   11/05/2015

ISBN: 978-1-5049-5839-4 (sc)
ISBN: 978-1-5049-5840-0 (e)

Print information available on the last page.

This book is printed on acid-free paper.

CONTENTS

ABOUT THE AUTHOR

Born in 1932, Wanda Harris Arnold (Wanda Gene) grew up in the Texas Panhandle and, as a child, witnessed the poverty, savage weather, and economic devastation of the Depression. These experiences shaped her life philosophy, which she imparted on numerous occasions to her children: "It's not what happens to you that's important; it's how you react to what happens to you." In the 1980s, she served as President General of the Daughters of the Republic of Texas, a reflection of her love of genealogy and history. She left one unpublished manuscript when she died in 2004. This is that story.

FOREWORD

When I started to the country school of Rock Creek in 1939, I stepped into a Time Tunnel. It could have been 1929 or 1919 or even 1909. Caught in the middle of the Great Depression, Rock Creek did not, could not, would not progress. It was a school where parents were entertained with a prejudicial skit about Blacks, where a teacher whipped a boy with a razor strap until he bled, where the girls picked dandruff from the head of the teacher while she was instructing, and where dangerous games such as Mumblepeg and Crack the Whip were played with abandon. Even the weather was captured in the Time Tunnel.

Although the era and system allowed the teachers to be despotic, the kids (not scholars, not even students—just kids) at Rock Creek were perhaps the fairest I ever met. There were no heroes or villains. There was no best athlete, most beautiful, or greatest scholar. The kids accepted me at face value. On the first day of school they showed me the cup at the windmill, and we all took turns drinking.

In later years when I attended schools not caught in a time tunnel, I began to realize how important Rock

Creek had been in chiseling my identity. My preschool years had been spent in a community where everyone remembered when my grandparents "first came," when my parents married, when I was born, and that I was an ONLY CHILD. I had a role to play, and I played it well. Life at Rock Creek, however, was ad lib.

Rock Creek died as did most country schools, all victims of stagnation. A few years ago I found myself wanting to return to the site of Rock Creek, wanting to enter the Time Tunnel, wanting to reminisce. I don't know what I expected to find. Certainly, it was not the pastoral scene of placid cattle contentedly grazing on green grass beneath a calm blue sky and billowing white clouds. Nor was it the electric and telephone lines bordering the paved road, belying the past. There was no vestige that Rock Creek ever existed. Not even a historical marker. I was overwhelmed with the feeling that a part of me had been buried in an unmarked grave.

As I slowly drove away from the site, I felt my jaw tighten a little. I knew I had to tell the story of a country school existing in the middle of nowhere during the Great Depression.

Wanda Harris Arnold
March 1996

AN IDYLLIC REALISM

The Depression years immediately prior to World War II were harsh, but they were innocent in their simplicity. I was the most sheltered of all farm children. I had life easy compared with others. Yet I grew up on realism. Sweat and blood. I saw more than I touched. I saw more than I heard. And I saw more than I smelled. But the smells are what I remember. And the blood.

We were cleaner than other farm families. My mother washed my hair every two weeks. I hated the washing with harsh soap and rinsing with vinegar. Vinegar smelled even after the hair was rolled. And it burned your eyes. We bathed once a week. It was quite a ritual. Daddy carried a bucket of water from the windmill. Mama heated the water in small stew pans. Then she poured the boiling water in a washtub on the kitchen floor. Daddy then carried in cold water from the windmill to cool the boiling water to bath temperature. Until I was thirteen, a few inches of water once a week in a tub was bathing. After my bath, Mama got in the same water for her bath. They put me to bed or made me turn my back, and Daddy bathed in the twice-used water. I brushed my teeth periodically. The same toothbrush lasted from birth through age nine.

We always had clean clothes to wear. Mama washed my socks and undies by hand every night. And I changed dresses every day. Daddy put on fresh work clothes every Monday without fail. And he worked in the fields all week. Hot, dirty fields. He worked hard, and his clothes got dirty, and sweaty, and stiff. He shaved once a week. His fingernails were never clean, even on Sunday.

Water was a priceless commodity. Someone had to carry it bucket by bucket from the windmill to the house. Mama had a rule that you had to drink every drop of water in the dipper. It was a "no-no" to throw away water that had been carried into the house. Everyone used the same dipper—friends and neighbors. Our school had only one dipper out by the windmill. A lot of the kids put the water back into the barrel. This was not a problem for me; that was Mama's problem.

No one ever washed their hands as a ritual at school or at home. At school there was no place. At home, it meant carrying in water, lighting the stove (also forbidden in summer), and then washing the hands. The reason that you didn't light the stove except at early morning or after dark was that there was no way to cool the house. That was in summer. Winter was different. The stove could be lit in the middle of the day. But we still didn't wash our hands, even in winter.

The migrant Mexicans who worked the farm suffered more than we did. More than the animals. When they came to the farm, they lived in the barn and were not given the privilege of using our outdoor toilets. But Mama was kind. She sent Juan, the sheepherder from Old Mexico, a piece of Jeff Davis Pie. I carried it in wax paper, and Daddy and I walked across the barnyard. I tripped and fell. Daddy brushed me off first and then the pie. Later, three families of Mexicans came to work on the farm during cotton season. Two families lived in the barn. One family lived in the car shed. Their children did not go to school. Gloria was the girl my age. She could do something that I could not do even though she had not been to school. She always spit blood when she coughed. And then one morning I looked out the back door and saw a fire up north on another farm. The Mexicans there were also living in a car shed. They burned to death. I wasn't there when they took out the bodies. Daddy was. Death and funerals were a part of growing up, but I never understood why they just didn't go ahead and bury the bodies instead of keeping them for several days. The ladies would stand over the casket with their fly swatters, keeping the flies off the corpse until it was buried.

I grew up on the smell of the barnyard. Granny had a scraper by the back door, and she would say to Poppy, "Lee, did you get all of the manure off your boots?" The smell of the chicken house and the smell of the outdoor toilet competed with that of the barnyard. On a farm, the barnyard, the chicken house, and the outdoor toilet had to be cleaned periodically. The men took care of this job. It wasn't "women's work."

I can remember the smell of the hot milk as the cows were milked. It was a sweet smell with the barnyard smell as the backdrop. There were flies, and the cows swatted them with their tails as they were being milked. And there were bugs. The bucket was on the ground in the barnyard. The cats waited during the milking for some milk. They inched closer and closer to the warm milk until Daddy yelled "Scat." When he was finished, the cats got their share. Daddy then took the warm milk into the house. There were often flies, gnats, and pieces of feed in it. Occasionally, the cow stepped in the bucket. Mama would strain the milk with a flour sack. Daddy then carried it to the windmill and placed it in the barrel of cold water. The milk was never boiled, but it was icy cold from the windmill.

Indoors were the smell of the slop jar and the smell of the slop bucket. A slop jar was what everyone used at night. There was only one. It was kept in the house until morning. The slop bucket was kept by the back door. It was the disposal. The cats and dog ate leftovers from our dishes. Mama then washed the dishes in a dishpan. I never really understood why since they were already clean. All scraps and dishwater went into the slop bucket. Even though it was covered, it smelled and drew flies. At the end of the day, Daddy took it outside to give to the hogs or chickens. Then he put the bucket back in place without washing or cleaning it.

It was fortunate that we were fairly healthy because we could not afford a doctor. Mama treated my colds by having me drink Vicks that had been melted over a kerosene lamp. When we didn't have Vicks, she used ten or twelve drops of kerosene on sugar every several hours.

Kerosene was also a remedy for toothaches—a cotton ball saturated with kerosene and applied to the gum. When I fell on the icy ground at the barn, I cut my knees on a rusty can. One knee needed stitches, but the doctor was distant and my parents were poor. Mama cleaned the blood from my knee with kerosene and bandaged it herself.

Farm animals did not have an easier life than the rest of us. Sheep were sheared. They were ugly after shearing, all naked with blood oozing from the numerous cuts on their bodies. Cattle were branded. They were tied. And they fought. That added another smell to the farm—the stuff they put on the cattle to heal the brand. The hogs were killed by hitting them in the head with the wrong side of the axe. Hogs were raised to be hit in the head. Other animals served other purposes. Hogs didn't. I loved the sheep and the little lambs. But they always cut the tails off the lambs. This hurt. And it was bloody. And they weren't playful for a few days after their tails were cut off.

Chickens provided endless diversion before they provided a meal. Poppy would take a chicken by the neck with one hand and start wringing it around and around. In a short time, the head came off, and he pitched it aside. The body of the chicken kept jumping for several minutes. There was no smell, but blood splattered everywhere. Mama had a slower method of torture. She was not strong enough to wring the head off the body, so she put the head under a stick and just pulled until it came off. Mama's method added frantic squawking to the blood. Granny was very fast at preparing the chicken. She gave the "innerds" to the cats, but they had to wait for those hot, bubbly, bloody "innerds" until she was finished. What the chicken had eaten was still inside. The cats did not always want to re-eat what the chicken had eaten—like grain and worms. The feet of the dead chickens could be turned into "toys." By pulling a tendon you could make them open and shut as a joke on people's arms and clothing or as an annoyance to the cats.

Chickens were a problem when it came a heavy rain. The mother hen couldn't save the chicks, and it was up to us to do it. The little chickens drowned very easily. We would chase them during a downpour, the chickens running in all directions. Occasionally, someone would step on a chicken. Squash—pronounced "sqush." That was it. Just sqush. A "squshed" chicken was not as ugly as a drowned chicken. Nothing was uglier than a drowned chicken. It was as flat as a sheet of paper. The method of reviving wet chickens was relatively simple. Mama put them in a large dishpan lined with an old sheet or towel. Then she put them on or in the stove. Eventually, you could hear "peeping" from the kitchen. Some never "came to life." Daddy would say, "That one isn't going to make it." The dead ones had to be thrown away.

Chicken eggs were another source of fun if you couldn't eat them. After Granny and Poppy had been away for several weeks, dozens of eggs in their chicken house had to be destroyed. We put them in buckets and went out by an old fence. You could feel the rumble inside the egg. When we threw the eggs at the fence, they exploded. Many of them had embryos, and the blood was milky in the yellow of the egg. The smell was the smell of all smells. Sulphur. We broke very egg without one exploding in our hands. And we left the egged fence to the flies and bugs.

Animals died frequently on the farm. One summer Poppy had a horse that died up in the pasture. We walked by him every day on our way to Granny's house. He was about forty feet from the path. At first he got all swollen. Then he exploded. The smell was terrible. Then came the flies, the animals, and the maggots. By the end of the summer, not much of him was left, and the smell had gone. I also had a dog that howled for two days and nights after it was kicked in the head by a horse. All one night I kept my head buried under the pillow. I didn't see him before he died.

When one of my cats got caught in farm machinery, Daddy told me that she would probably be dead when I came home from school. She wasn't. She lost her tail, and one leg was badly mangled. She bled for several days and then began to heal. Red lived a long life and was the best cat we ever had. Some of her kittens did not fare as well. There was an enormous male cat that came to kill the kittens one by one. You could hear the thud of the pounce and then the horrible noise from the kitten when it was caught by the jugular. It died a quick death. It was bloody, and so was the porch. I decided to save the rest of the kittens and waited for the big tomcat, but he was faster than I was. He dropped the next kitten as I ran out the door yelling at the top of my lungs. I carried a bloody, gurgling, half dead kitten to a place of comfort so that it could live a day before dying.

Mice were everywhere—inside and outside. Every time Daddy moved his shocks of feed, there would be mice and rats. The cats caught the adult mice and played with them. If there were baby mice, Daddy finished them off with the heel of his boot. Once, one ran up his leg on the inside of his pants. Very calmly he grabbed the outside of his pant leg and squeezed the mouse to death. Then he shook his leg, and the dead mouse fell out. The cat picked it up and carried it away. Mice also lived inside the walls of our farmhouse, which was easily accessible because the facing on the door didn't really fit. It had to be pried out from the wall with a clothespin for the door to shut properly. This left an opening, a narrow slit, right in the top of the door facing. One day a mouse was running back and forth in the wall. Every time it got to the door, its tail would hang down. Finally, Mama had enough. She removed the clothespin, but she caught the tail of the mouse as it was hanging down. The mouse squealed and squealed. So she picked up her scissors and cut off its tail. It was free, and it still lived in the wall.

Blood on a farm was a normal part of daily living. When Daddy and some of his friends kept seeing an eagle by Tule Canyon, they shot it and brought it back to the farm. Its wingspan was six feet, truly a magnificent bird. Mama wanted to make a picture, and it was my duty to hold up its head and pose it. Its head was cold and bloody, the cold blood soggier than warm blood. It stuck to my hands, and so did the feathers that were matted in it.

It was a simple life. I lay in bed and considered my family. Mama was afraid of certain things. Daddy wasn't afraid of anything. And he loved everyone. Well, almost everyone. I was certain he wouldn't allow former President Herbert Hoover in the door if he should happen by. Daddy held him personally responsible for the Depression. Yes, it was a simple life, but I was happy.

Wanda Gene at one year old with her parents

"IT WAS TIME TO
START TO SCHOOL"

"It was time" for me to start to first grade. Farm families did things "when it was time." We didn't have appointments—even to see a doctor. We didn't live by a schedule, and we didn't have a desk calendar. We did things "when it was time." When it was time to plant, Daddy planted. When it was time to harvest, Daddy harvested. When it was time to cook, Mama cooked. Now it was time for me to start to school. I had been seven since May.

Mama had loved going to school, and she was eager for me to experience the same enjoyment. I wasn't eager. I didn't feel any emotion. It was just time to start to school. I had learned my ABCs from my blocks. And I had learned to print capital letters and spell from those same blocks. Mama had gone to school in New Mexico where the students purchased their textbooks. She had taught me to read from her first and second grade readers. Arithmetic was part of our routine conversation:

> "If we had one cat and she 'found' five
> kittens, then how many cats did we have?"

> "If two died and one ran away, how many
> cats were left?"

I am grateful that Mama savored her schooldays. She taught me and motivated me to learn.

I was going to Rock Creek School, an eight-grade country school in the adjoining county. I had never seen the school, the teachers, or the students. Since I didn't have any anticipation or expectation about the school, I was not disappointed when I first set eyes on Rock Creek. The schoolground was barren. It was just dirt, hard dirt. Not newly-plowed dirt or sandy dirt. Hard dirt. Newly-plowed dirt, with its softness and freshness, invites you to hold it in your hands until it slowly trickles through your fingers. Or, it encourages you to take off your shoes and wiggle your toes in it. Sandy dirt, left when the topsoil has washed or blown away, beckons you to put it in your mouth like tobacco, "chawin' and spittin'." The dirt on the schoolground was as hard and as uninviting as the times in which we lived.

The schoolhouse was in the center of the schoolground. There it sat—Rock Creek School—on top of the barren schoolground. I have seen pictures of country school buildings nestled in the midst of lush grass, colorful wildflowers, and shady trees, with vine-covered walkways, curved driveways, shiny flagpoles, and a plethora of play equipment--swings, slides, merry-go-rounds. But Rock Creek School was a desolate building in a desolate landscape. A number of years earlier, the school had been painted white. Although the paint was not yet peeling, the building seemed to promise that the process could commence at any moment. The building depicted the farm people of the Depression, people who had endured just about as long as they could without "peeling."

There were sparse patches of brownish-yellow prairie grass beneath some scraggly trees on the northeast corner of the schoolground. On the southeast corner, there was a windmill with its barrel of ice-cold, fresh-running, drinking water. We all drank from the same cup. There was no place to wash our hands—anywhere. The two-hole outdoor toilets were at the back of the schoolground, one for the girls on the northwest corner and one for the boys on the southwest corner. Since the school could not afford toilet tissue, the toilets were well supplied with magazines and catalogs, the Sears catalog the most common of these. The three-room teacherage and the supply house were in the schoolyard just south of the school building. There were no pavements, no sidewalks.

The inside of the building was as austere as the outside. There were two identical classrooms, each with its own dark, minuscule room for coats, lunches, and everything else forbidden in the classroom. There were two walls of blackboards and one wall of large, low windows, without curtains or shades to block the afternoon sun. The blackboard at the back had unreachable, bare windows above it. The wall in the front of the room was a folding partition, separating the two classrooms. It was also bare. The floors were wood, and there was no floor covering.

The schoolroom contained only the bare necessities. There was an enormous wood/coal-burning stove in the corner by the windows. The teacher's desk was in the front of the room. There were four short rows of desks with fold-up seats. The top of each desk had an indention for pencils in the center and an inkwell on the top right-hand corner. Beneath the top of the desk, there was a shelf for the Big Chief tablet, books, and cigar box of crayons, pencils, and scissors.

There were no luxuries at Rock Creek. There was no electricity and there was no plumbing. There was no telephone and there was no radio—no communication with the outside world. There were no flag, no play equipment, no musical equipment, no library, no interest center, no clock, and no school bell. There was not even the overly-familiar picture of George Washington.

And that was it—Rock Creek School.

Mr. and Mrs. Biggs were the teachers. She taught the lower four grades in one room, while he taught the upper four grades in the other room. Since they weren't local people, there was an air of mystery as to why they would choose to teach at a country school in the middle of nowhere. Mr. Biggs, noticeably older than she, would have been unidentifiable in a crowd. He appeared stern, strict, rigid, and grim. His unsmiling, almost-frowning countenance was not inviting. On the other hand, Mrs. Biggs was the epitome of a storybook teacher—black hair, colorful makeup, chic dresses, shiny jewelry, and spike heels. Understandably, the older girls admired Mrs. Biggs, and she seemingly enjoyed conversing with them. As for the younger children, the ones of us she taught, Mrs. Biggs was totally unapproachable.

Not only did Mr. and Mrs. Biggs teach four grades simultaneously, but they had complete responsibility for the buildings and grounds. This meant carrying wood and coal, shoveling ashes, cleaning blackboards, burning trash, sweeping and dusting the classrooms, and supplying the outdoor toilets with catalogs. Had there been an occasion for medical attention, Mr. and Mrs. Biggs would have served as doctor and nurse. Although the teachers were responsible for the maintenance, they did not always do the work themselves. The older boys were responsible for many chores.

Teaching in a country school was a full-time task, a demanding and thankless task, with meager pay. Mr. and Mrs. Biggs salvaged some relief from this harsh structure by "disappearing." At recess and noon they remained in the school or teacherage while we played. As soon as school was dismissed, they went to the teacherage while we waited for the bus to come from town with the high school students. On Friday, they drove away from the schoolground promptly at 4:00 p.m., leaving grades one through eight totally alone for thirty to forty-five minutes.

The students, a term used loosely, at Rock Creek were hearty farm kids who had known no life except the Great Depression, the era when people majored in the basics. Twenty-six kids, sixteen boys and ten girls, enrolled in the eight grades at Rock Creek, expecting to learn no more than the "3-Rs" of Readin', 'Ritin', and 'Rithmetic. "College," "Preparing for the Future," and "Career" were never mentioned. Rock Creek students expected no frills, and they received none.

My introduction to the school, teachers, students, and parents was at the short enrollment-day orientation. Most of the pupils and their families knew each other; we were newcomers—outsiders. It was comforting to have Mama sit with me at a desk. I found myself inching closer to her so that I could feel the comfort. Only then did I begin to look around the room. That was when I saw "It." I quickly looked away, assuring myself that I had a vivid imagination. Then I cast a quick glance in the same direction. "It" was Walter Bean's nose.

Walter had a year-round allergy that caused exceptionally thick, whitish-green mucus to drain from his nose. The snot, usually fresh but sometimes crusted, was always there—hanging from his nostrils to the top of his lips. Just before the mucus parted and curled around his mouth like a mustache, Walter would lick it off. No one ever seemed to try to help him solve his problem, or even notice it.

When the enrollment was over, Mama stood up and turned up the seat, unaware that she had caught my fingers until I began to cry in pain. Embarrassment overwhelmed me when everyone, including Mrs. Biggs, stared in my direction, but I couldn't stop crying. I was still sniffling as we drove away. This was the first omen of the year to come.

The school year began 28 August 1939 and concluded 10 May 1940. Since most of the kids had to pick cotton, one six-week recess was allotted for "cotton pickin'." This left five six-week periods—150 days of school. Actually, there were only about 120 days of school due to the number of impossible-attendance days when all twenty-six kids were absent. Even the threat of a heavy rain, bad sandstorm, or violent blizzard would be sufficient reason for the bus to take us home early. If it rained during the night, we knew the bus would not run. No one could maneuver the stick-shift, power-steeringless vehicles on the dirt roads that became instant mud bogs in wet weather. Regular attendance was an impossibility and no one fought it. Not even the school system. There were no make-up days for bad weather.

The year was short by modern standards, but a day at school was long for a first grader. I rode the bus to school, arriving about 8:15 a.m. Although our classes did not start until 9:00 a.m., the bus had to deliver the high school kids to Silverton before that. In the afternoon, both Silverton and Rock Creek dismissed at 4:00 p.m., and we had to wait for the bus to come from town before we could start the long trek home.

I suppose everyone's first day of school is memorable. Mine was. The school day began without ceremony. We didn't have flags—inside or outside. No one had ever heard of the Pledge of Allegiance. I was in the sixth grade before I knew of the Pledge. We didn't sing "The Star-Spangled Banner" or "Texas, Our Texas." I doubt that anyone knew the words. Rock Creek didn't even begin the day with the customary Bible reading or prayer.

Mrs. Biggs assigned me the first desk on the first row. When I looked to the right, I saw a blackboard. When I looked straight ahead, I saw nothing but a bare partition. When I looked to the left, I saw Walter Bean and his nose. We were forbidden to look behind us. When I looked down, I saw a repulsive desktop. My desk was knife-scarred. Someone had carved his initials, his friends' initials, and his enemies' initials in the top of the desk. I had always been most particular with my things, and now I had been assigned the ugliest desk in the room.

The format of the day was simple. When Mrs. Biggs called "Fourth Grade Reading," the fourth graders went to her desk and read. Then it was "Third Grade Spelling" at the desks and "Second Grade Arithmetic" at the blackboard. After an interminable time of "First Grade Nothing," I heard Mrs. Biggs instruct one of the older students to find the flash card "Spot" and the first grade reader "Spot." My time was coming. When Mrs. Biggs called me to her desk to show me my new reader, I had my first glimpse of a book with a picture of a black dog with one white spot.

Pointing to the obvious spot on the dog, Mrs. Biggs condescendingly quizzed, "What could be his name?" I couldn't decide how to handle the "Spot" situation, how to tell Mrs. Biggs that I had overheard her tell the student to get the "Spot" book, that I knew the name of the dog, that I knew the name of the book. Since I didn't think I ought to make the teacher look irresponsible or careless, it seemed that my only recourse was to play dumb. When I responded with "Blackie," she told me to look more closely. After studying the picture intently, I queried, "Whitey?" I was becoming increasingly agitated, wondering how I could halt this nonsense. Glancing at Mrs. Biggs, I considered telling her that she had tipped her hand and that we should shuffle the cards and begin again. Later, I learned I was fortunate in not telling her of her error. She pointed to the white spot on the dog again, and with relief, I timidly answered, "Spot?" Mrs. Biggs was pleased that her method of teaching had been successful. I was also pleased because she wrote my name in the book, telling me that it was my first reader.

Recess was next. No one bothered to tell me that it was recess. Since everyone removed their lunch sacks from the coatroom, I assumed that it was time to eat. I was the only girl in first or second grade, but the older third and fourth grade girls made a place for me to sit with them on one of the thin patches of prairie grass. Chattering and giggling about events of the previous year, they opened their lunch sacks to remove the morning recess snack. Unable to enter into the conversation, I opened my lunch sack and ate my entire lunch. Just before Mr. Biggs appeared and called "Books," one of the girls observed my empty sack and asked cynically, "You didn't think it was lunch, did you?"

After lunch, which was really morning recess, Mrs. Biggs sent the second graders to the blackboard for Arithmetic. And she sent me. She gave us detailed instructions:

"Put down 7. Then put another 7 beneath that one.

Now draw a line. What is 7 plus 7?"
I was panic-stricken. Here I was on my first day of school, and I had no idea what she meant by "7 plus 7." Obviously disappointed in me, Mrs. Biggs was rather sharp:

"If you had 7 apples and bought 7 more apples, how many would you have?"

I felt the smile of confidence on my face:

"Do you mean 7 AND 7?"

I beamed. She gave an audible sigh and nodded. I proudly wrote "14" and realized that I had learned a new word—"plus."

When Mrs. Biggs dismissed us again, the kids returned to the coatroom for their lunches. I wasn't hungry, but I was embarrassed when I realized I had eaten my lunch at recess. I watched the others eat their lunches of bread—white bread, biscuits, or cornbread—and meat— chicken, pork, or steak left over from supper. There were no vegetables. Their extras were boiled eggs and pickles. During the remainder of the year, I had similar bread and meat. My extra was dessert, Philadelphia Red Cake or Jeff Davis Pie. Once Mama placed cold biscuits covered with sugar and butter in my lunch, and SHE called it "dessert." Although I ate the dessert, I must confess that I seriously considered leaving the biscuits in the sack to blow away with the rest of our trash.

It would have been "wrong" to let the biscuits blow away. The sack was of no concern. No one "wasted" food during the Depression. On the other hand, we dropped our napkins, wax paper, and sacks on the ground, where they lay until the wind took them. Not one of us could have defined "litter" as it is used today.

The lunch period lasted an hour. After the girls finished eating, they invited me to join them in their play. Walking with them to the back of the supply house, I was confronted by a sight worse than my disfigured desk. Utilizing boards and rocks, the girls had carefully marked out a floor plan of a house and had furnished it with broken pans and dishes. I had always preferred playing outside to inside. The girls wanted me to pretend to be inside a house. It just didn't make sense to me. Having been tied to a desk all morning, I wanted the freedom of the outdoors. I did not share the enthusiasm of the other girls for pretending to be inside. That was the last time I ever played "house."

Mr. Biggs emerged from the school, yelling "Books." I returned to the classroom and reflected on the morning. Mrs. Biggs had flunked reading. I had flunked recess. I had excelled at second grade arithmetic. And I had an ugly desk. That wasn't too bad for my first half day.

The afternoon was broken only by recess and Stoney. When Stoney, a boy in Mr. Biggs' room, came into our room to empty the wastebasket, he stopped at my desk, leaned over, smiled at me, and whispered, "What are you drawing?" I responded in a hushed voice, and he left. Immediately, Mrs. Biggs called me to her desk, demanding that I tell her what he had said. I was afraid not to tell her, but I thought it unfair for her to make me betray a private conversation. I probably could not have defined "tyrant," but this was my first introduction to one.

The most beautiful sight in the world that day was Mama and our big dog Dynie waiting for me to step off the bus. Although the bus let me off a mile from the house, not a single day passed all year without Mama and Dynie meeting me. Mama didn't look like most farm women. She had a wide-brimmed, white hat that had been a Sunday hat. She wore long gloves. The hat and gloves were to keep her skin white and soft. She had on nice pants and high-heeled dress shoes. Mama changed her attire to match the seasons, but she always looked immaculate after walking a mile on a dirt road. The bus driver had a rule that we must be standing at the door by the time the bus stopped. Thus, I always heard him talking to himself under his breath when he saw Mama. I never knew what he was saying. If he said anything to me, it was, "There she is." I don't think he ever noticed the dog.

If anyone had asked me what I learned on my first day of school, I would have responded "Plus." And had I been asked the same question about the first year at school, I most likely would have given the same answer. Yet, no year fortified me for life as did my first year in school when I learned invaluable lessons in responsibility, self-reliance, patience, and reflective observation. Although there were times when I would have greatly preferred learning at home, my parents had been right. "It was time" for me to start to school.

Wanda Gene on her first day of school at Rock Creek

Wanda Gene and Dynie

"WAIT 'TIL AFTER COTTON PICKIN'"

"You'll have tuh wait 'til after cotton pickin' tuh buy. . ." was a profound statement, a statement of blighted dreams and hailed-out anticipations, spoken by those who all too often had seen last year's labor and next year's income swept away just prior to harvest. The fears and hopes for the coming year were expressed in those terse words "wait 'til." There were times when farmers knew months in advance that their crops would not "make," knew that they would have to tighten their belts one more notch. Their "wait 'til" was next year. For some, "wait 'til" was now. Time sputtered, stalled, and ground to a halt, as the farmers who had good cotton in September awaited the verdict. Fear, born of common sense, gripped them when they thought of spending money that would not, could not be replaced. The farmers looked at their families and said, "Wait 'til after cotton pickin'."

I was going through my own lean days in first grade, and I wasn't optimistic about my future. Imprisoned in a schoolroom of drudgery and tedium, with Mrs. Biggs serving as the strict warden, I found time standing as still for me as it was for the farmers. I could only "wait 'til" the six-week reprieve of cotton pickin'.

During my first week of school, I discovered there were not many ways to break the monotony of sitting long hours with nothing to do. As frequently as I dared, I asked for permission to go to the windmill to get a drink of water. On one such excursion, I lingered far too long, watching whirlwinds play in the field across the road. The weather was "right" for the frequent formation of whirlwinds—still, hot, dry. The whirlwinds were hopping and skipping, playing chase, and appearing and disappearing with unusual rapidity. It was a weather phenomenon to make one linger.

Unwillingly, I dragged my feet toward the building, unaware that a whirlwind had leapt the fence and was rushing toward me. The Whirlwind engulfed me, swirling dirt, gravel, and debris against my face and legs, stinging them like an angry swarm of insects. Resembling a mischievous child, The Whirlwind snatched my bonnet from my head and sped away. Without plan or thought, I chased The Whirlwind. Since whirlwinds were whimsical, following no charted course, I had no idea where it might take my bonnet. Without realizing it, I had run across the road, through the barbed-wire fence, and into the field. In its mad rush to get away from me, The Whirlwind dropped my bonnet on the plowed ground. It was only after I rescued my bonnet that I felt the barbed-wire scratches on my arm.

When I realized where I was and how long I had been gone, I raced toward the school like a sprinter seeking to win a medal. I did not want Mrs. Biggs to come out of the building in search of me and find me in the field across the road. Timorously, I entered the room, fervently hoping Mrs. Biggs would not remember how long I had been gone. She walked toward my desk, suspiciously peering at my flushed face and scratched arm. I didn't think she could hear my wildly beating heart. Abruptly, she wheeled around and marched away. Although I was extremely thirsty, it wasn't the time to ask for permission to go to the windmill again.

Mama had loved her teachers. I knew that I was supposed to love Mrs. Biggs. So I did. But I didn't. Mama was much prettier, and she loved me. She had taught me, and she was proud of me when I learned. Soon after the whirlwind episode, Mrs. Biggs gave me another glimpse of her disposition. While waiting for the bus after school, I learned to spell "Halloween." I was pleased, and I thought she would be equally pleased. Although we were forbidden to bother Mrs. Biggs after school, I knocked on the door of the teacherage to tell her of my accomplishment. She only partially opened the door, but I heard her eyes threaten, "This had better be urgent." Disconcerted, I stammered my now-unimportant news and fled, hearing the door slam behind me. Mrs. Biggs was NOT Mama.

After the incident at the door of the teacherage, I tried to practice the maxim "out of sight, out of mind." It was not always possible. Late in the afternoon on the day before the break for cotton pickin', Mrs. Biggs summoned me to her desk. Looking at her inscrutable face, I had no clue as to what I had done to attract her attention. Her words were a total surprise:

> "I think it's time for you to be in second grade. You'll need to learn to write 'longhand' while you're home. And you must read this book. If you'll do those two things, I'll put you in second grade when we come back from cotton pickin'."

I began to jump, run, wave, shout, and clap—on the inside. Outwardly, I calmly nodded my head and accepted the book.

The book Mrs. Biggs handed me was on phonics, a tool being discontinued in many schools. Fortunately, Rock Creek could not afford to discard any book. Although Mrs. Biggs had told me to "read" the book, I "studied" it daily. Phonics was more than Readin', 'Ritin', and 'Rithmetic. It was a "plus."

I could hardly wait to learn to write "longhand." Big kids "wrote," but little kids "printed." None of us had heard of the word "cursive." Since Rock Creek didn't own any penmanship books, the task of teaching me to write fell to Mama or Daddy. They had a lengthy and weighty discussion on who was to form the letters I was to copy because they wanted to make the right decision for my benefit. Finally, they decided in favor of Mama, who made plain, legible letters, as opposed to Daddy, who "fancied up his writin'."

I practiced my longhand on leftover, government forms. Although Daddy was a farmer, he also worked for the AAA, one of President Roosevelt's New Deal programs. Every night I watched Daddy intently as he sat by the kerosene lamp, painstakingly filling out forms and drawing maps. Usually, I was in bed long before he blew out the lamp. In the morning I would find a small stack of leftover forms on my table. I hoarded the forms, being careful to use them only when I was ready to try my best longhand.

It was time for twenty-six kids and two teachers to return to school following cotton pickin'. We had spent our recess in various ways. The majority of the kids had picked cotton. Since teachers received no remuneration during cotton pickin', Mr. and Mrs. Biggs had probably left Rock Creek. Although I had played, I had also studied phonics and learned to write. I found myself with a sense of confidence and eagerness lacking in my first six weeks of school. Feeling much older and wiser, I knew that the mistakes of the first six weeks would not be repeated.

When I arrived at school, Mrs. Biggs promoted me to second grade, without inquiring if I had read the phonics book and learned to write. I soon forgot her lack of interest in my accomplishments when I began to reap the benefits of second grade. Mrs. Biggs moved me from the first grade row to the second grade row. I had a smooth desk, and Walter Bean was behind me. I fervently hoped he didn't sneeze. Next, she gave me my new books. The only subjects I had actually studied in the first grade were Arithmetic and Reading. Now I had Arithmetic and

Reading <u>plus</u> Language, Writing, and Spelling. Finally, she spoke the words that unlocked the door of monotony, making me a trusty at Rock Creek:

"Any time you want to join the third and fourth grade classes when they recite their lessons, you can. Oh, yes, you can also watch the girls use the hectograph."

The hectograph, which belonged to Mrs. Biggs, was a copier—messy, time-consuming, but, nevertheless, a copier. It was a tray filled with purple gelatin, sometimes purchased and sometimes homemade. The original, whether a picture or words, was traced with indelible ink and then placed on the gelatin until it "took." A copy was made by laying a blank piece of paper on the gelatin, sponging the top with a wet rag, peeling the paper from the gelatin, and spreading it to dry. Each copy was lighter than the previous one. After all the copies were made, the image had to be removed from the gelatin by water or heat. It was a "purple" task—purple copies, purple hands, and sometimes purple dresses. This was not boys' work, and Mrs. Biggs rarely directed the girls when they were using the hectograph. She had less time-consuming methods for teaching classes at Rock Creek.

History was not a "lesson" in grades one through four. It was learned from the calendar. Although we did not celebrate most of the days, Mrs. Biggs explained the background and significance:

October 12, Columbus Day
November 11, Armistice Day (pronounced "Ar-<u>mis</u>-tice")
November, Thanksgiving
December 25, Christmas
January 19, Robert E. Lee's Birthday
February 14, Valentine's Day
February 22, George Washington's Birthday
March 2, Texas Independence Day
April 21, San Jacinto Day
June 2, Jefferson Davis' Birthday
July 4, Independence Day.

School dismissed for the summer in May.

Farm kids did not need to study Health. "Everyone" knew farmers were healthy. No one at Rock Creek had heard of sanitation. We could go to the outdoor toilet OR to the windmill on one excused absence from class. We could not go to both. Had we gone to the windmill at noon or recess to wash prior to eating, we would have had to dry our hands on our clothes. Although we did not know drinking from the same cup at the windmill was unsanitary, I must admit that I never drank immediately after I had seen Walter Bean at the barrel.

Language was . . . well, Language was a subject that we attempted to study at Rock Creek. The Language book told us about adverbs, tenses, predicates, and diagrams. However, we had our own grammar, colloquialisms, idioms, and cant, all more descriptive and picturesque to us than the staid sentences, unimaginative words, and non-descriptive expressions in the book. I have wondered how the proud author of our Language book would have reacted had he heard some of the expressions we used at Rock Creek. We understood:

"I seen et."
"She larnt me my lessons."
"I done et (ate) et."
"He hoped (helped) me."
"He throwed the ball good."

The kids knew when to use "Aint" and when to use "Haint." Although I had a number of Great "Aints"— "Aint" Georgie, "Aint" Maggie, "Aint" Callie, I didn't have any Great "Haints."

No teacher or book could have changed the "Rural West Texese" dialect of the 1930s. We spoke it fluently. A speech teacher once told me to hold my nose while I repeated the alphabet. According to her, the only letter I should feel in the lower part of my nose was "n." With my Rural West Texese, I could feel all twenty-six letters of the alphabet, and some letters not in the alphabet.

The unwritten rule for pronunciation in Rural West Texese was to change the enunciation of all vowels until they were nasal. "Drink" and "think" became "drank" or "dreenk" and "thank" or "theenk." The long "o" followed by "w" as in "shadow," "pillow," and "window," became "er" as in "shadder," "piller," and "winder." "Friday" and "Saturday" were "Fridee" and "Sadurdee." "Fire" and "hire" were "fawr" and "hawr." An "s" in a contraction such as "isn't" and "wasn't" became a "d" as "idn't" and

"wudn't." "I wudn't kiddin' whin I sed thet I thank I
wont a drank. Everwho wonts innythang else, jist lemme
know" translates to "I wasn't kidding when I said that I
think I want a drink. Whoever wants anything else, just
let me know." Another maxim was to change one syllable
words into two syllable words by the addition of the suffix
"uh." Thus, "I want a drink of tea" became "I wont a
drank-kuh uv tea-uh."

Miz Biggs worked us aplenny in Language class. We
wawr plumb askeart thet our-uh heads would-uh bust-uh
with all she had dun larnt us. Oops! Thus, we were always
glad when she decided to conclude the Language session
in favor of Third Grade Reading.

As the days grew colder, Mrs. Biggs relaxed the strict
rules that had governed us in the fall. She moved from her
desk in the front of the room to a chair beside the wood/
coal stove. When she called a class to her chair to have a
lesson, she allowed the other kids to move into the vacated
seats to be closer to the stove. On extremely cold days,
she permitted the students to sit two to a desk—but NO
talking. It was during Fourth Grade Geography on one of
those cold, blustery days that some of the girls volunteered
to help Mrs. Biggs remove the dandruff from her hair. I
must admit that watching the fourth grade girls scratch
for dandruff was much more interesting than listening to
them answer questions on what was growing in China.

Spring was an anomaly at Rock Creek. In a season
of newness, we returned to the routine normalcy of the
fall. There was no more camaraderie with Mrs. Biggs. The
freedom to move from desk to desk was gone. Discipline

was strict and punishment was harsh. To add to our misery, the spring winds all too frequently picked up the loose topsoil and hurled it at us grain by grain in a sandstorm.

The sandstorms at Rock Creek were not the same as the dust storms (dusters) of the early 1930s. The sandstorms were "our" sand, while the dust storms were "their" oily, dark dust, "rollin' in" from an area extending from the Dakotas to the Texas Panhandle, an area known as the "Dust Bowl." Those who endured the dust storms remember how they turned day into night until people lit coal oil lamps at midday. The women spread newspapers on their tables, beds, and other furniture, but it took only a few short hours for the dust to sift into the open houses and completely bury the print on the newspapers.

Oblivious of our plans for the day, the sandstorms muscled their way into our routines. They harassed us when they blew, and they vexed us when they departed, leaving their sand, grit, and grime clinging to our faces and hands, settling in our water buckets, crawling under our fingernails, and decorating everything lying in a horizontal position. At Rock Creek we found ourselves constantly rubbing our thumbs across the tips of our fingers or rubbing our hands on our clothes to rid ourselves of the dirt. We ran our tongues around our teeth to dislodge the grit in our mouths. The perpetual sandstorms of the spring of 1940 began to "git to us."

Occasionally, the sandstorms became hazardous. Daddy was cautious, knowing all too well the danger of a blinding sandstorm. When he was in such a sandstorm, unable to see beyond his radiator cap, he stopped the car to "find" the road. Amazed and shaken, he discovered his car was far off the road, almost touching the pumps of an abandoned "fillin' station."

It was only a few weeks after the "fillin' station" experience that Daddy realized another "bad 'un wuz in the makin'." He rushed home from work, picked up Mama, and drove to school to rescue me. In the rush to get to school, they did not notice the bizarreness of the storm. Usually, the sandstorms were straight winds of high velocity, causing tumbleweeds to roll like a ball until thwarted by a barbed wire fence. The pile of tumbleweeds against the fence would grow higher and deeper until finally, fence and posts fell together like comrades in battle. This sandstorm was different.

Daddy began to shake his head in disbelief at the eerie damage done by the wind and tumbleweeds. The sandstorm was not a straight wind. It was as though it were alive, "breathing"—exhaling, inhaling, exhaling, inhaling. The tumbleweeds piled up and the wind enabled them to work on the fence "steeples" (staples) holding the wire to the posts, just like a child works on a loose tooth, back and forth, back and forth. As soon as the tumbleweeds neatly extracted the "steeples" from the posts, mile after mile of wire fell to the ground, intact, leaving the naked fence posts standing without even a tumbleweed to hide their shame.

When the sandstorms diminished in frequency and intensity, we beheld a magnificent sight. Seas of wheat, still more green than yellow, covered the brown landscape. The wheat, planted in October, had imperceptibly sprouted, grown, and headed, despite the odds presented by the heartless weather. The farmers would have to wait for the ripening of the wheat. School would be out before the farmers told their families what they were beginning to think, "Better wait 'til after wheat harvest to. . ."

My life paralleled the wheat. It was as though I had been planted in October when I was promoted to second grade. I had gone through my own long growing season, changing, growing, maturing so slowly that no one, not even I, was aware of it. Factors, not always pleasant or ideal, had challenged and threatened my growth during the year. It was not yet time for harvest in my life. Until then, we would have to "wait 'til. . ."

The teacherage at Rock Creek

Wanda Gene at the beginning of second grade

WHEN AUTHORITY
BECAME TYRANNY

The flat, barren prairie with its warm, half-dead grass gave no indication that the world was in turbulent upheaval. Our Depression Era farm home, serene, tranquil, and harmonious, denied the very existence of totalitarianism. Thus, when I entered the kitchen in September 1939, I stopped in utter incredulity. Mama was huddled over the radio just as she would have huddled over a hot stove on the coldest of days. She was intently listening to a staccato voice, a voice that never breathed, speaking a language I had never heard. When The Voice finally paused, there was a crescendo of "Heils."

The Voice began again, shrieking at me, dictating that I stand frozen to the linoleum. Mama broke its grip on me when she glanced up and all too hurriedly assured me, "Don't worry. It's war. But it's a long way from here—all the way across the ocean. And we are free." Then she huddled over the radio again, forgetting my presence. I was relieved to escape before The Voice grabbed me again. Outside, I sat on my favorite patch of prairie grass and thought about things far beyond my comprehension. I knew there were more people shouting "Heil" than I had ever seen at one time. But how many were there? The twenty-six kids at Rock Creek certainly could not make that much noise.

And I didn't know where "a long way from here" was. My world was large—to me. I could look in all four directions and see the sky touch the ground. Was "a long way from here" beyond the point where the sky touched the ground? I had traveled. Amarillo and Snyder were 215 miles apart on Highway 87, and I had been to both. Although I had never been west of Highway 87, I had gone as far as seventy miles east without seeing an ocean. Whatever was happening was far beyond the ocean and my world. Looking across the endless, flat, barren land of my world, I convinced myself that The Voice could not slip up on us. And if it did . . . well, Daddy could handle anything.

"We are free," Mama had said. I doubt that anyone could have explained freedom to me. Freedom meant freedom to play. At home there was unparalleled freedom with no brothers, sisters, or neighborhood children to thwart my decisions on what and how and where and when I was to play. In the first weeks of school, I discovered that I was free to play as I chose. We played before school—without direction or supervision. We played for thirty minutes at the morning recess, an hour at noon, and thirty minutes at the afternoon recess—without direction or supervision. We played thirty to forty-five minutes after school—without direction or supervision. We were so unaccustomed to the presence of the teachers that we didn't even realize they were gone.

Although we didn't discuss it, we knew not to abuse our freedom at play. We had our own Law of the Playground. We certainly didn't want to invite the strictness of the classroom to the schoolground. Our differences were settled without benefit of a mediator. No one whined:

"Thar's nuthin' tuh do."
"That's no fair."
"No one'll play with me."
"Ya never play the games I wanna play."

We played without benefit of predetermined fitness goals or physical education classes. Sometimes we all joined in one giant game. At other times, several different games were played simultaneously in large groups or small groups. Grades did not have to play together, nor did they have assigned play areas. No one had to play at all if he so chose.

Admittedly, we had to play games that didn't require special equipment. My uncle attended a country school in another county. The surrounding schools in his county challenged the others in basketball games on hard, dirt courts. His school even had uniforms for boys and girls on two age levels. Not us. We didn't have uniforms. We didn't have a court. We didn't even have a ball. His school also played softball. Although our ground was as hard, flat, and smooth as artificial turf, we couldn't play softball. Rock Creek could not afford a ball and bat.

The only time Rock Creek engaged in an organized, competitive team sport occurred when the boys of Gasoline School challenged the Rock Creek boys to a game of football. There wasn't much warning, and there wasn't much practice. Rock Creek didn't have helmets or pads or uniforms. Certainly, Rock Creek didn't have any goal posts. There is a strong possibility that Rock Creek didn't have a football. What the Rock Creek boys did have was the courage to accept the challenge from Gasoline.

Most of us had never seen a football game. And, of course, there was no TV. Mama told me about her girlhood experiences in the cheering section at basketball games. My contribution to the football game was to teach the girls one of Mama's yells:

Rickety, Rackety, Russ
We're not allowed to cuss
But jammety jell
We're gonna yell
For Rock Creek School or bust.

If any team was ever "whupped up on," it was the Rock Creek football team. They were bruised, skinned, battered, AND humiliated. Only in hushed voices did the girls discuss the 55-0 trampling by Gasoline. That was the beginning and end of organized sports at Rock Creek.

Following a long morning or afternoon of classroom monotony, we filed outside at recess or noon with seeming nonchalance. Once beyond the rigid routine of the school, we were free to play. And play we did. Like ravenous wolves attacking their prey, we devoured the moments of playtime. Calls echoed across the playground:

"'Red Rover'—over here."
"How 'bout 'Three Deep'?"
"House! House!"
"Wolf Over the River!"

And so we scattered like leaves in the wind to enjoy our favorite game.

"Wood Tag" was invigorating relaxation. Someone was "It," and the rest of us touched wood to be "safe." This was easier said than done on a schoolground without trees or shrubs. We provided our own wood, scattering scraps of kindling from the woodpile. There was a time limit on how long we could remain on a piece of wood. If two of us ran to the same piece of wood, "It" could tag one of us. When I was first introduced to the Rock Creek game of Wood Tag, I thought it would be a good idea to carry a piece of wood in my pocket. Shaking his head, one of the boys took me aside and with simplicity clarified the rules, "Nup."

Tired of Wood Tag, we would start across the schoolground to join a game of Red Rover already in progress when someone would suggest, "Hey, let's 'Crack the Whip'." Joining hands, we would run as swiftly as we could. The first one in line would stop, swinging the line in a large arc. The ones on the far end had the most fun as they found their legs moving faster and faster until they were "flying." In a few short years, schools branded

Crack the Whip, sometimes known as "Pop the Whip," as dangerous due to the supposed "whiplash."

Rarely a day passed that some of the girls didn't "Jump Rope." In the 1930s jumping the rope was done for fun and not for fitness. We had a short piece of farm rope, with "just right" stiffness. Willingly, we took turns throwing the rope and jumping the rope. I learned "front door," "back door," "hot pepper," and "high water." We also jumped to the favorite rhyme:

> Rich man, poor man, beggar man, thief,
> Doctor, lawyer, merchant, chief,
> Tinker, tailor, cowboy, sailor,
> Butcher, baker, candle maker.

Marbles—"Funsies," but not "Keepsies," and "Mumblepeg" were usually played by the boys. Mumblepeg was played with pocket knives. Most farm boys, even those in the first grade, carried knives to school. A farm boy of the 1930s would not have been caught without his knife any more than a girl today would be caught without her purse. When the boys found some dirt with the right hardness, they would kneel in a small circle and open the sharp gleaming blades of their knives. In turn, each boy would carefully take his knife, place the blades at various angles, and competently flip his knife. Points were given for the degree of difficulty of the toss and for the specific blade that stabbed the ground. No one was ever blinded, scratched, or even nicked in a Rock Creek game of Mumblepeg. All too soon, Mumblepeg joined Crack the Whip in the list of banned games at schools.

The cold of winter conquered our schoolground, forcing us to retreat inside the building for our play. While the older kids were enjoying the social games of "Winkum" and "Spin the Bottle," I was learning to play "Jacks." I had found MY game. Understanding my love for Jacks, Mama and Daddy gave me a gift when it wasn't even Christmas or birthday—six steel jacks and a rubber ball that was truly "alive."

I practiced Jacks at home. Sometimes Mama and Daddy played with me. At first I worked on the basics of throwing the jacks, tossing the ball vertically without letting it land on the jacks, and dissecting the jacks in the correct sequence. Then I progressed to practicing "babies," "easies," "pigs in the pen," "eggs in the basket," "downs," "ups and downs," "ups and ups," "downs and ups," "downs and downs," and "around the world." At school my jacks were always within reach, although they should have been stored in the coatroom, and the kids knew they could depend on me to produce the jacks the moment we were dismissed. Our games lasted for days during the winter months, as we continued from recess to noon to recess.

Spring, with its influx of sandstorms, might have come unannounced had it not been for the unexpected blossoming of "Stilts" on the barren schoolground. Kenneth Lee was the first to arrive at school with his homemade stilts, long thin stilts just thick enough to hold his weight. In awe, we watched him mount his stilts and streak across the schoolground like an ostrich. By the end of the week, the other boys had made stilts of every shape and fashion, from thin and tall to fat and short, from splintery rough to silky smooth. None were painted, blending into our world in perfect harmony. Some of the boys lumbered about like elephants, while others were as lithe as cats. No one was as skilled as Kenneth Lee. I, too, had my opportunity to walk on stilts at Rock Creek. With kindness and patience, Kenneth Lee frequently lifted me up on his tall stilts, firmly holding them steady as I pretended I was racing across the ground.

The inevitable happened. It was Friday afternoon, and the Biggs had left school early, as was their custom. Kenneth Lee was by the windmill, taking long strides on his stilts. Donald Joe, a boy my age, and I were following. Quite unexpectedly, Kenneth Lee stumbled. Briefly, he struggled to gain control of his stilts. Unable to maintain his balance, he jumped from his stilts, letting them fall. One of the stilts swept across Donald Joe's face, not hurting him, but bloodying his nose. Kenneth Lee helped me as I wet my handkerchief in the water barrel to wash Donald Joe's bleeding nose. When the bleeding stopped, Kenneth Lee resumed his stilt walk, with Donald Joe and me hard on his heels. It seemed like an insignificant incident.

On Monday morning I stepped from the bus at school to be greeted by glum faces: "Kenneth Lee's a-havin' tuh chop up all the stilts, cuz he het Donald Joe." I couldn't believe it. In the first place, it had been an accident with no major consequences. I was there. I was an eyewitness. In the second place, no one at Rock Creek would have "told" a malicious story on Kenneth Lee. Certainly, Donald Joe's parents hadn't caused the trouble. They wouldn't have said a word if Kenneth Lee had taken his stilts and deliberately "whomped" Donald Joe from behind. No, some unseen and unnamed source was working in our lives.

The severity of the punishment suggested a sequence of events. I had heard whispers that some of the parents objected to the early departure of the teachers on Friday. One of the kids probably mentioned Donald Joe's bloody nose to his parents. It would have been easy to spread the message at Rock Creek Church on Sunday. The trustees were the ones who governed the school and the teachers. The stilts incident gave them a valid reason for objecting to the early departure of the teachers. When reprimanded, the teachers vented their anger and frustration on Kenneth Lee and the stilts we enjoyed so much. The teachers never again left early on Friday.

It was a dreadful morning. Wretchedly, I sat at my desk, biting my lip, blinking back my tears, trying to swallow with an enormous hen's egg in my throat. Kenneth Lee was behind the supply house and we couldn't see him. But we knew what was happening. It was one of those rare days at Rock Creek when there was not a breath of wind, and Mrs. Biggs had opened the windows. Unsparingly, relentlessly, mercilessly, we had to listen to the rhythmic chop . . . chop . . . chop of the axe. Whenever there was a pause in the chopping, we agonized all the more, knowing that Kenneth Lee was selecting another splendid pair of stilts for unwarranted execution. Decisively. Irrevocably.

Chop . . . chop . . . chop. The methodical sound continued like the no-quarter beat of drums from a totalitarian general's army. At last Kenneth Lee emerged around the corner, walking ever so slowly toward the school building, dragging the axe behind him. We thought he had finished the dastardly task.

None of us was prepared to see the rigid Figure of Authority marching toward Kenneth Lee. Mr. Biggs displayed no compassion, no understanding, no gentleness. Although we could not hear the words, we knew by the punctuated gestures of Mr. Biggs that he was reiterating the sin of making stilts. Kenneth Lee stood motionless, apparently absorbing the words of Mr. Biggs, but intently watching the toe of his brogan dig a hole in the ground. Concluding his lecture, Mr. Biggs jerked his head in the direction of the woodpile, and the two disappeared around the corner of the supply house. Helpless and defeated, we could only sit in class, waiting, listening, watching. Time seemed nonexistent. An eternity later, we heard "It" again—chop . . . chop . . . chop. Mr. Biggs was making sure there would not be a shred of evidence that Rock Creek had ever enjoyed stilts.

I hurt for Kenneth Lee. He had brightened all of our lives when he brought his stilts to school in a spring of sandstorms. I hurt for the other boys. THEIR stilts. Their stilts had been condemned and executed in one mass judgment. I hurt for me. Never again would Kenneth Lee firmly hold his stilts, letting me walk around the schoolground. I hurt for the school. More than the stilts had been destroyed.

We had all been taught to have the utmost respect for Authority. But late in the Spring of 1940, Authority suddenly became Tyranny. Tyranny didn't belong at Rock Creek. It belonged to The Voice "a long way from here." Nevertheless, Tyranny had invaded and conquered our flat, barren prairie. And worse, we hadn't even seen it coming.

Mr. Biggs   Mrs. Biggs

THE CODE OF THE
THREE MONKEYS

Destitute farmers watched the assets of a bygone era disappear with rapidity during the collapsing years of the Great Depression. Nothing was inviolate—jobs, farms, banks. In later years people reminisced, "We lost everything except our pride." The morals and values were among the few survivors of the past. And thus, the people grabbed and clung to the old code of prudishness and conventionality taught by their grandparents. The Code was illustrated in books by the three monkeys, one with hands over eyes, one with hands over ears, and one with hands over mouth. The mandate was simple, but direct: "See no evil, hear no evil, speak no evil." The Rural West Texese version said: "Shh! Ye jest don't talk 'bout thangs like thet."

The Code of the Three Monkeys dictated our thoughts, words, and actions. Abiding by The Code made one a "lady" or a "gentleman." Only the uncouth and vulgar dared challenge the validity of this spiritual and moral philosophy. It was a suffocating code, rigidly governing our lives at home and at school, relentlessly forcing us into a world of ignorance, submission, fear, and yes, pride—pride that we had kept The Code with honor.

The Code required that we be able to control our enthusiasm, uncertainty, and inquisitiveness at all times. Although I knew The Code well by the time I was three, I did not always contain myself. Once, without thinking, I pointed at an interesting scene in the pasture: "Look! Look! That cow is riding the other one." Gently and kindly, Mama explained without explanation, "We mustn't look at things like that. And we mustn't talk about things like that." Although I frequently peeked at this oft-repeated farm scene, I could only wonder what I was observing.

By the time I was five, I could look at my parents and know when we were under The Code. Since we didn't own a car, we were with Granny and Poppy in town late one Saturday afternoon. Although Daddy and Poppy kept mentioning that it was nearly time to go home to perform the routine nightly chores, they made no move to leave. Finally, Daddy pulled his watch from his pocket, studied it for a moment, and then said to Mama, "You about ready?" She nodded. Turning to me, he said, "Come on." Granny and Poppy remained in the car, not asking where we were going or when we were returning. But they knew. Mama and Daddy chose not to reveal our destination or purpose to me. Glancing at them, I knew this fell under The Code. I didn't ask questions. It didn't take us long to walk to the building adjacent to the Court House.

A man wearing a badge opened the outside door of the building. We followed the man single file up some narrow, dimly lit steps. At the top of the landing, a sleepy, yellow cat yawned at us. As the man opened another door with a key, he said to Daddy, "Call me when you're ready to go." Daddy's brother was extremely delighted that we had come to see him. Since I had heard the key turn in the lock when the man shut the door behind us, I knew that I could not go play with the cat. I hoped Mama and Daddy would not visit long.

At last Daddy stood and called through the bars. To my relief I heard the key turn in the lock. We descended the steps in single file, following the man with the key and badge. The yellow cat was stretched out, asleep on a step. "Don't bother the cat. Step over him," Daddy admonished. It concerned me greatly that a cat would sleep in a building in such close proximity to a door that a man could lock and unlock. I considered "accidentally" nudging him, but I did as I was told.

We then returned to the car where Granny and Poppy were waiting. Normally, Granny would have asked me where I had been and what I had done. She acted as though I had not been gone. No one ever discussed, explained, or mentioned our visit to the County Jail. I knew The Code of the Three Monkeys. I had not "seen" what my eyes told me I saw.

One would think that nothing in church would fall under The Code, but it did. The preacher read his Scripture from Philippians 1:8: "For God is my record, how greatly I long after you all in the bowels of Jesus Christ." I had heard a new word, and I was anxious to learn its meaning. After we arrived home, I asked my question, "What are bowels?" Mama and Daddy looked at me, and then at each other, and then at me again, in disbelief and embarrassment. I waited expectantly as Mama told Daddy to answer my question and Daddy told Mama to answer my question. When Daddy left the room and I had no answer, I knew that once again I had broken The Code. Mama showed her usual patience and kindness, saying, "You will know when you are older. But you must be careful about the questions you ask."

By the time I entered Rock Creek, I had a graduate education in The Code of the Three Monkeys. While the experiences of the other kids might have differed from mine, their catechism had been the same. The overall principle was to refrain from mentioning "personal" words and subjects. We could not ask personal questions, and we could not share personal feelings. This tended to limit our conversation because few subjects were impersonal. If someone forgot The Code, we all had the responsibility of reminding, "Shhh. We jest don't talk 'bout thangs like thet."

There was an unwritten list of general words and topics that were forbidden: sex, menopause, menstruation, pregnancy, birth, suicide, retardation, finances, politics, religion, divorce, "privates" (genitals), masturbation, and surgeries such as hysterectomies and hernias. No one had heard of "homosexuals" or "rape," or these would have been on the list. And there was a Rock Creek list of subjects that were taboo: Walter Bean's nose, Mr. Davis' drinkin' problem, Willis Smith's runnin' away from home at 14, Mr. Corn's weeds, Mr. and Mrs. Biggs' past, and Kenneth Lee's stilts.

The greatest weapon of The Code was fear—the fear of hurting or embarrassing someone with words, the fear of becoming a social pariah, the fear of receiving lecture or punishment. Thus, we adhered to our training in deafness, blindness, and silence. At Rock Creek, we studied, played, AND kept our mouths and minds closed. There is no better illustration of The Code at work at Rock Creek than in discipline and punishment.

All during the year of first/second grade, I observed punishments, both harsh and humiliating. Although punishment was obvious, I had to pretend that it had not happened. I could not ask, "What did he do?" Had I broken The Code, I would have been punished in identical fashion. I could not even sympathize, "I'm so sorry for you." Solitary confinement was never more solitary than punishment at Rock Creek. Mr. and Mrs. Biggs did not "Yank the Hair" or "Drag Across the Room while Twistin' the Ear" as did some teachers. The most frequent punishments at Rock Creek were "Sittin' on the Wall" and "Puttin' the Nose in the Ring."

The first punishment of the year came in the form of The Wall. While Mrs. Biggs was teaching Language to the fourth graders standing around her desk, she suddenly looked harshly at Billy Jack in the back of the room. "Go sit on the wall," she sharply instructed him. Billy Jack knew what to do. He had been at The Wall before. Walking to the wall, he placed his back against it, sliding down until he was in a sitting position. It was as though he were sitting in an invisible chair. This was not the last time I saw someone Sittin' on the Wall.

The Wall produced several fears for me. Although I was afraid that I might be punished with The Wall for an unknown sin, I had greater apprehension over breaking my pencil lead at an inopportune time. The pencil sharpener was located in close proximity to the place of punishment, and I didn't know how I could step over the one Sittin' on the Wall to sharpen my pencil without "seeing" him.

The first Puttin' the Nose in the Ring punishment of the year followed soon after The Wall punishment. Since Mrs. Biggs was always busy, directing four grades at one time, I was amazed when she focused her attention on Jane, sending her to the blackboard alone. Instead of waiting for further instruction, Jane stood on tiptoe, drew a circle, and put her nose in it. This became another familiar sight. The Ring brought its own set of fears to me. I found it difficult to close my eyes to this punishment if the one standing to my right at the blackboard during second grade arithmetic was Puttin' Her Nose in the Ring instead of subtracting. An even greater anxiety was not knowing if I could ignore the aftermath of Walter Bean's standing with his nose in The Ring at my assigned place at the blackboard.

Not once . . . not once did I know what occasioned disciplinary action by Mrs. Biggs. I could not ask. Mrs. Biggs did not explain. No one dared volunteer the information. It was frightening not knowing what I might do to bring down the wrath of the teacher. I practiced

Sittin' on the Wall and Puttin' My Nose in the Ring at home. I wanted to do well if I ever had to be punished in such a manner.

My fear of judgment grew with time. I knew my day would come. And it did. While I was busily engaged in watching the boys at Mumblepeg, Betty Ann began to annoy me, hovering over me, breaking my concentration on the game, wanting . . . something . . . I don't know what. In exasperation, I turned toward her and popped her bare arm with my wet handkerchief that I had just soaked in the water barrel. When I saw Betty Ann "tunin' up," I was sorry that I had hurt her feelings, although I knew I hadn't hurt her physically. I no longer felt sorry for her when I saw her running to "tell."

I wondered if I were prepared for the inevitable punishment that would surely come. The Ring? Yes. The Wall? Yes. But what if . . . what if it were "The Whippin'" like Edward's whipping? The Whippin' occurred early in the fall, establishing the authoritarian rule of the teachers and testing the strength of The Code. Regrettably, Edward, one of the older boys, was the one who paid the price.

Near the end of the school day, Mr. Biggs dispatched one of the girls to our room with a message of obvious importance for Mrs. Biggs' ears only. Immediately, and without explanation, Mrs. Biggs dismissed class for the day, hurrying us out of the building. As we stepped into the bright sunlight, we were met by the dismal faces of the kids from Mr. Biggs' class. I had no idea why school had been dismissed or why everyone looked so glum. In later years I would have thought that it was a fire drill, but Rock Creek didn't have fire drills. Some of the older kids whispered a few words to those standing next to them. And then without anyone moving his lips, the word was passed from person to person, spreading like fire across a dead prairie:

"Eddard is gonna git uh bustin'."
"You mean a lickin'?"
"Yeah, a whippin'."

Although they told us what was going to happen, no one offered an explanation of the "sins of Eddard." I felt myself trembling, afraid to ask any questions.

A Whippin'! Mr. Biggs had a leather razor strap hanging in his room, and we had all seen it. It was an awesome strap. I couldn't imagine anything worse than Edward being alone with Mr. and Mrs. Biggs—and that leather strap. Years later I was told what happened at a whippin'. I am glad that I didn't know on that day at Rock Creek. The teacher would command, "Grab the ankles," before commencing the lashing. In some instances the student was made to pull down his overalls to insure the strap could be felt. As frequently as not, a good whippin' drew blood. Both the number and the force of the "licks" were at the sole discretion of the Figure of Authority. The pupil who received the whipping was expected to "take it like a man." In fact, he was often told, "This will make a man out of you."

While Edward was whipped, we waited. Nothing else seemed fitting. On any other day, free time would have been turned into playtime. No one suggested a game. All twenty-five of us tried to crowd onto the small porch close to the door of the school. No one had the courage to venture away from the security of the other kids or the building. It was as though the schoolground were filled with vultures, rattlesnakes, and coyotes, while the school was filled with the giant razor strap that grew larger in our minds as we waited. As I stood in terrified submission, another fear gripped me. I wondered if Mr. Biggs whipped girls—little girls.

After three or four eternities, the door banged open with a forceful crash, jolting us to attention. Edward appeared first, followed by Mr. Biggs. Mrs. Biggs was standing in the background. We bowed our heads, not wanting to humiliate Edward by staring at him, not wanting to incriminate ourselves by acknowledging him, not knowing what to do. Feeling that I was hidden from the eyes of Mr. and Mrs. Biggs, I dared cast a furtive glance at Edward. His face was flushed, and his jaw was set as though it had not relaxed after the last lash. His eyes were fixed on an indefinable "something" in the distance. Involuntarily, my eyes followed his. All I could see was a vast expanse of nothingness.

Unknowingly, we had parted like the Red Sea in front of Moses and the Children of Israel as we stepped back to permit Edward to walk between our lines. Still, no one uttered a word. Mr. Biggs was the one who broke the silence, speaking harshly to Edward's sister, "Make sure your Daddy hears about this." She quickly bobbed her head up and down in assent. I thought it was a difficult burden to place on her. Authority had dictated that she tell on her brother. And everyone was thinking the same thing: "Edderd'll git a worse lickin' whin he gits home and his old man knows what happened at school." The rationale of the Era made little sense to me: "If you are punished at school, then you are guilty; if you are guilty, then you have disgraced the family; if you have disgraced the family, then you will be punished at home more severely than at school."

After Edward had run the gauntlet of our lines, he just kept walking across the schoolground, down the road, walking . . . In panic, I thought he had just quit school for good. Then I realized that the Biggs had dismissed school for the day in order to give Edward a whipping, and Edward lived within walking distance of school. He was a lonely figure in his colorless shirt, patched overalls, and scuffed brogans, shuffling down the rut-filled road, kicking at the hard clods of dirt. His sister and a few other kids followed, none walking with Edward, none talking to him. The incident was never mentioned again.

Mrs. Biggs snatched me from my reverie of Edward and The Whipping when she came around the corner of the building, demanding, "Where is Wanda Gene?" She was trailed by a self-satisfied, non-hurt Betty Ann. Angrily and resentfully, I followed Mrs. Biggs into the building. It was with surprise that I heard her say, "Put your head on your desk for the rest of recess." I did as I was told, but I began to cry, audibly sniffling, punishing her for listening to a tattler, for listening to one who had broken the Law of the Playground. When I peeked at Mrs. Biggs, I was pleased to note that she was becoming increasingly uncomfortable with my crying. I turned up the volume a notch, but I didn't win. Mrs. Biggs rapped her pencil on the desk and made an emphatic statement: "That's enough. Hush!"

When the kids began to come in after recess, I felt embarrassed that I was at my desk instead of at The Ring or The Wall. They didn't see me. I was invisible. They were not allowed to "see" someone who had been punished. No one ever mentioned "Staying in for Half of Recess" to me. Words . . . any words, would have been helpful:

"What did Mrs. Biggs do to you when she got you inside?"

"We missed you at recess."

"I am sorry."

Even "You were wrong" would have acknowledged that I existed. Nothing. Just nothing.

Our world, asleep like the yellow cat on the winding steps of the jail, was voluntarily imprisoned by The Code. No one challenged The Code. It was as though our world were repeating Daddy's admonition about the cat, "Don't disturb it. Step over it." I don't know if other kids had as many smoldering questions, ever growing in number, as did I. The Code said, "Don't ask." And no one did.

The two-room schoolhouse at Rock Creek

"It Weathered a Lot"

An "outsider" might think the expression, "It weathered a lot," meant the routine conditions of rain, snow, wind, and sand. Oldtimers knew the statement encompassed the violent weather experienced in The Wind, The Cold, The Blizzard, The Downpour, The Drought, The Electrical Storm, the Hailstorm, or The Tornado.

The weather was not only violent, but it was sudden. I was particularly vulnerable when the change in weather affected the roads. In 1939, Briscoe County didn't have one inch of paved roads. In fact, the "Texas Almanac" reported that the county had spent only a little over $6000 on road improvements during the previous year. Daddy could be working forty miles away, totally unaware of the weather at Rock Creek, totally unaware that I was in danger of becoming rainbound, sandbound, or snowbound at school.

The Depression Era weather forecasts were highly inadequate. KGNC in Amarillo gave brief local predictions several times a day, but never interrupted a scheduled program. The 5,590 residents of Briscoe County, sixty miles from Amarillo, were not included in the area weather forecasts. The printed word was of little help. The news was a day old before it was printed in the newspaper and two days old before the mail carrier delivered the paper to our rural mailbox. Although the "Farmer's Almanac" and "Black Draught" calendar were reliable for determining the phase of the moon, the time of sunrise and sunset, and the zodiac signs used by many farmers, they were questionable when predicting the day by day weather a year in advance.

Daddy became our weather forecaster out of necessity. The first thing he did every morning was look at the windmill. The fan showed the direction of the wind. The wheel suggested the velocity, although only a farmer could have made the calculation based on how he had "set" the wheel. Relying on his windmill and his John Deere thermometer, Daddy would predict:

"Wind's from the west. It's gonna be a bad 'un (sandstorm)."
"It's from the north. It'll snow before night."
"Not a breath of air. It'll be a scorcher today."

If the weather appeared threatening, Daddy would announce, "I'm going outside to 'study' the clouds." I would go with him to do my own "study." Clouds that looked frightening to me were dismissed with, "Aw, they're gonna scatter." Obvious rain clouds or hail clouds were observed with disappointment or relief, "They'll go 'round us." Low rolling clouds accompanied by rumbling thunder were described by Daddy as "downright booggery." When

I was alone, I studied the clouds intently, wondering how Daddy interpreted their secrets.

Although I didn't understand the clouds, I understood the cold. We were introduced to our new foe, The Cold, the day we moved to the Rock Creek area in January 1938, the day Mama and Daddy "put up" the stove and "hooked up" the radio. The Cold possessed every inch of the house, and we were the invaders seeking to drive it away. Wrapped in my warmest clothes, I joined Mama and Daddy in the living room to watch them prepare their inadequate weapon, a small kerosene stove, to attack The Cold. They assembled the long black sections of stovepipe, measuring, lengthening, shortening them until the stove pipes tightly connected the stove and flue. With satisfaction, Daddy carefully poured the kerosene into the stove, pulled a wooden match from his pocket, struck it on the side of his pants, and lit the stove. While I waited for The Cold to flee, Daddy began "hookin' up" the radio.

"Hookin' up" the radio required more expertise than "puttin' up" the stove. With The Cold numbing and stiffening his fingers, Daddy managed to position and attach the outside antenna. The radio sat on a crocheted doily-covered table in front of the window. Beneath the table, the ugly car-sized battery glared at us. Daddy concluded his task by wiring the radio, battery, and antenna together. By this time the living room should have been warm. It wasn't. The Cold was still in control. Although Daddy recorded in his diary, "Put up stove/hooked up radio," he knew it had been futile. The following day, Daddy recorded in his diary, "Moved stove and radio to kitchen." The Cold had won. We retreated to the kitchen where we lived for four harsh winters. We ate in the kitchen. We dressed and undressed in the kitchen. We bathed in the kitchen. We played games in the kitchen. We did everything in the kitchen except sleep.

At night, not even the kitchen was sacrosanct from The Cold. As soon as Mama and Daddy turned off the stove, blew out the lamp, and went to bed, The Cold stealthily crept into the kitchen, repossessing it. One of its routine acts was to freeze the drinking water in the bucket. Even after Mama and Daddy lit the kitchen stove in the morning, The Cold dawdled in defiance. The Cold controlled the living room, the playroom, and the empty room 100% of the time and the kitchen at night. We governed the kitchen during the day. The bedrooms were "No Man's Land," with us in possession of the beds and The Cold possessing the rooms.

At bedtime, I undressed in the kitchen and ran on the cold floor to my cold bedroom, followed by Mama with a scorching-hot blanket to wrap around my feet. She then crushed me with a high pile of homemade quilts, leaving only a tiny airhole for my breathing. The Cold was waiting, pretending it was defeated, seeking an opportunity to creep into bed with me the minute I was asleep. Although The Cold never succeeded in dislodging the warmth of my bed, it had its day of vengeance when it destroyed my favorite knickknack on a shelf in my room. On my birthday I had received a small, glass, water-filled dome. I was intrigued with the birds that gently floated around until they landed near two children playing on a sandy beach. No one thought The Cold would touch the water dome as readily as it touched the water bucket. One night The Cold froze the water in the dome, leaving a time bomb to detonate when the water thawed. I did not discover the malicious deed of The Cold until it was too late.

At times The Cold made a cruel alliance with The Wind and The Snow, begetting a family of Blizzards. Between 8 April 1938 and 16 February 1940, we lived in "Blizzard Alley." The Blizzards attacked from the north, coming straight across the prairie, with nothing between the North Pole and us to obstruct their growing force. They picked up every lonely "critter" and "thang" in their path, hurling them with fury into the cracks and chinks in the house. Accompanied by the rattling and creaking of the windows, the imprisoned "critters" and "thangs" uttered their incessant squeals, moans, and groans. Sometimes they howled in solo and sometimes in chorus, but always at fever pitch, mercilessly continuing until The Blizzard decided to leave.

On 8 April 1938, Daddy recorded in his diary that The Blizzard had blown sixty miles an hour from the north all day. The outside doors of the house did not fit. Cold came in. Dust came in. And on that day, snow came in. Mama, Daddy, and I were in the kitchen playing games, as was our custom on bad days, totally oblivious to the snow accumulating in the living room. Although the living room was on the north facing The Blizzard, it had the protection of a porch, roofed and closed in from waist down. On that day, nothing, especially a mere porch, could block the wind and snow. The Cold made a rare mistake in freezing the snow sifting into the living room, instead of letting it melt on the floor. Daddy reported in his diary, "Shoveled two (wash) tubs of snow from the living room." The Blizzards continued the following winter, but with less intensity. The prelude to the grand finale began Christmas Day 1939 and continued intermittently for two weeks. Daddy shoveled a path for my new bicycle, but it was a vain effort. No sooner had he finished his work than it began to snow again. The snows continued with little break into February.

No one knew that "weather was comin'" on 16 February 1940. Daddy went to work. I went to school on the bus. The "granddaddy of all blizzards" hit suddenly and ferociously. As soon as Daddy realized what was happening, he rushed home from work, picked up Mama, and started toward Rock Creek. The roads were already blocked. Returning home, Mama and Daddy began walking in the driving wind and snow, struggling only to the Gregg's house, two miles away. They could go no further. Dismally, they returned home, fighting The Blizzard, not knowing where I was. I could be at school. And then again I could be on the bus, stranded in a drift.

None of us at Rock Creek paid much attention to the gathering storm. We had all seen "weather." The day began overcast and gray, a typical windy, wet, and cold day. Before noon, the temperature began to drop, the moisture became snow, and the wind "picked up." In a short time, all we could see through the windows was white. It was like a white sandstorm. The kids began to whisper that it was impossible to make it all the way to the outdoor toilets. My first realization of the enormity of The Blizzard came when it was my turn to go outside. It was a foreign world. Within five feet of the schoolhouse, there were drifts much higher than my head, blocking my view, hemming me in. Strangely, the drifts left a path like a track field encircling the building. The Wind was extremely rude, biting my face, trying to push me down. I did not tarry.

In early afternoon the Biggs dismissed school, allowing the kids living within walking distance to make hurried exits. A few families came for their children in their cars. The rest of us waited for the bus. It never came. Although Mr. and Mrs. Biggs had been planning to leave on the weekend, they did not leave us alone at school. They couldn't. I don't remember when we realized that we were snowbound—three girls, seven or eight boys, and Mr. and Mrs. Biggs. None of the kids worried. Or complained. Or cried. We accepted our plight without reaction, waiting patiently for the Biggs to make some decisions.

Heat and light were the lesser problems. Mr. Biggs had moved his class into our room to conserve the wood and coal the boys had been carrying in all afternoon. Even though it was cold on the far side of the room, we were more than comfortable standing around the large school stove. Mr. Biggs produced one kerosene lamp, but the darkness barely noticed. In the flickering dimness, I watched our enormous shadows move about the room like dark ghosts. Feeling the unearthly howl of The Wind, I moved closer to the group at the stove.

The major problem was that Mr. and Mrs. Biggs had no food for ten children. When Mr. Biggs told us that he could walk to the store two miles away to purchase food, Carl Ray, a strong boy, volunteered to accompany him. I was glad I was small and female. After an elaborate ritual of "bundlin' up," Mr. Biggs and Carl Ray disappeared into the whiteness. I do not know how long they were gone, but it was long enough for us to be relieved when they returned. Certainly, it was perfect weather for hot chili and crackers.

When it was time for bed, Mr. Biggs informed us that he and the boys would remain in the school, sleeping on their coats, while Mrs. Biggs and the three girls would go to the teacherage. As soon as we arrived at the teacherage, Mrs. Biggs put us to bed in our clothes on a foldout couch. After our hot cereal in the morning, Mrs. Biggs quickly herded us out the door while she remained in the teacherage. We were awed by the scene as we walked from the teacherage to the school building. The storm was gone, and so was our world. It had disappeared beneath the snow. There weren't even any fences in sight. None of us had ever seen mountains, but the drifts were mountains of snow with their peaks touching the roof of the teacherage and school. The Cold was biting, and The Sun—The Sun was shining brightly as though nothing had happened.

As soon as Mama and Daddy arrived at the Gregg's house on Saturday morning, Mr. Gregg joined Daddy to attempt a four-mile walk to rescue Zonelle Gregg and me. Although the snow had stopped, head-high drifts and knee-high snow frustrated their efforts to blaze a trail. Mr. Biggs saw them struggling through the snow toward the school. Turning to Zonelle and me, who were busy at Jacks, he said, "Who are those men walking toward us?" We paused long enough to look out the window. "Our Daddies." Then we returned to Jacks. Exhausted and famished, Daddy and Mr. Gregg arrived at school in time to join us for a lunch of hot chocolate and marshmallows, a meal that did little to refuel them for the trek ahead.

I must confess that I was a little embarrassed when Daddy came into the school. Having just celebrated his thirtieth birthday, Daddy was handsome, wearing his clothes with flair, especially his hats and shoes. On that day he had on his "everday" overcoat, heavy rubber boots that he wore to the barnyard, and a cap with earflaps and goggles. I couldn't believe that Mama had let him come to school dressed like that. The worst was to come. He had brought me all the "old" clothes that Mama could find, including a leather overcoat that had belonged to my uncle. And I had to stand there while all the kids watched Daddy wrap me in layer after layer of worn-out clothes.

We had not reached the edge of the schoolground before I realized that this was going to be a most difficult journey. Mr. Gregg and Zonelle started ahead of us. I was to follow Daddy, stepping in his tracks. But Daddy was tall, and his tracks were far apart. The fences and gates were covered with drifts, and we had to climb over them. Occasionally, the wind would swirl snow in my face. I wanted to lie down in the snow, waiting until Daddy picked me up and carried me. Suspecting this, Daddy urged me on, "You can make it." It required three hours to struggle two miles to the Robinson farm. As soon as Mrs. Robinson saw us coming in mid-afternoon, she began to cook ham, potatoes, gravy, biscuits, and cobbler. I wasn't hungry, but Daddy was starved. It was with great relief that I learned that Mr. Gregg and Daddy were planning to leave Zonelle and me at the Robinson farm overnight.

As Zonelle and I sat on the floor in front of the coal fire, I smugly produced my jacks, which "I" had rescued from being snowbound. Happily, we continued the game we had begun at school. We should have stopped playing when Mr. Robinson collected the ashes on the ash pan, leaving the bottom door of the stove open. Before he could return to close the door, Zonelle made a bad toss of the ball, letting it bounce into the open door of the stove on top of the smoldering ashes. Although we were able to rake the half-burned ball from the ashes, we could no longer play Jacks. For the first time during The Blizzard, I felt an overwhelming surge of homesickness.

On Sunday morning, Mr. Gregg and Daddy followed the plans to go with Mr. Bean in his wagon to Rock Creek to get the three Bean boys and then on to the Robinson farm to pick up Zonelle and me. I was ready to start the final trek home—until I saw Mr. Bean in his horse-drawn wagon carrying the boys. It was beneath my dignity to ride in a wagon. They had done that in the "olden" days. And then I noticed I was going to have to sit by Walter Bean and his nose. I hesitated. Daddy didn't. Before I knew what was happening, Daddy lifted me high in the air and placed me in the wagon beside Walter.

We reached home at last, but we were still in a topsy-turvy world. For days Daddy had to kneel, reaching DOWN into the barrel by the windmill to draw water. I walked OVER the gates and fences, enjoying it immensely when it was play instead of the urgent necessity to reach the Robinson farm. Mama, Dynie, and I climbed a high drift, laughing as my tall Daddy looked UP at us. It was the time of year when I should have been IN school, but I was OUT. For two weeks we played games and ate snow ice cream—a mixture of snow, whole milk, sugar, and vanilla.

The Wind, The Cold, and The Snow had united forces to hurl a savage bombardment at us. Time would have freed us from the results of the fury of The Blizzard, but Caterpillars speeded the process. We readily joined the liberation parade of farm families following the Caterpillars into town, where there was only one topic of conversation. Newcomers and those "still wet behind their ears" spoke with awe, "I've never seen it weather like this," while the oldtimers remonstrated, "Ye oughter been here in 1918."

Surely, there had been a lifetime of weather! But, "It weathered some more." A gentle rain would have offered a welcome respite from The Sand, The Wind, The Cold, and The Blizzards. But the rains were not always gentle. Daddy's terse words in his diary speak volumes:

"Mr. Fields struck by lightning."

"Went to funeral for Mr. Fields."

"Hail got all of new cotton."

"Rained five inches in an hour."

"Rain and wind blew down wheat."

"Tornado hit us."

After school was out for the summer, Mama and Daddy took me to Granny's house for a week's visit. When they were ready to travel the twenty-five miles home, we casually waved to them, totally unaware that ominous and portentous weather was brewing.

The next morning, we heard the news that a tornado had hit Kress and then traveled on across the country to Clarendon, killing and wreaking devastation. Poppy immediately left for the barn to worry alone. Granny and I looked at her large county map of Texas, tracing the path of The Tornado from Kress to Clarendon. Our house was obviously in the path. Granny, always honest and matter-of-fact with me, expressed her concern, "Well, they may have blown away." I nodded in agreement. All we could do was wait.

Mama and Daddy had not arrived home until bedtime, having stopped to visit with friends. As a part of the bedtime routine, Daddy latched the back door, not to provide a measure of security, but to keep the door closed. Since the ill-fitting door did not "catch," Daddy had attached a latch to the doorframe with a long nail. The first gust of wind blew the latch and nail from the doorframe, slamming the door open against the wall. Mama and Daddy awakened with a start, saying in unison, "The back door." Daddy bolted toward the door in the total darkness, Mama pattering after him. He was yelling, "Don't step on the nail!"

Daddy barely managed to force the door closed before The Tornado hit in force. Both Mama and Daddy were leaning against the door, feeling the repeated surges of power attacking them from the other side. They were fighting The Tornado in a house that could not keep out cold, sand, rain, or snow, at a door that wouldn't stay closed on a calm day. The voluminous roar pounded their ears and their wildly beating hearts pounded their chests. "It" lasted a lifetime and was over in a minute. There was no way to survey the damage. It was pitch black and raining in torrents. Feeling "as weak as kittens," they returned to bed to wait until morning. Once in bed, Daddy began to laugh. Mama had always been afraid of storm cellars, but during The Tornado, he heard her say, "If I had a cellar tonight, I would jump in."

Mama and Daddy were up at daybreak, not knowing what to expect. As a matter of habit, Daddy glanced toward the windmill. It was gone. The Tornado had sucked it out of the ground without damaging the six-foot holes or the six-foot posts of the windmill that went in the holes. As a parent would lay a sleeping child in bed, The Tornado had gently laid the windmill intact on its side in the garden. The roof of the barn was twisted askew, but all the animals were safe—even the young chickens. The crops were ruined. Mama and Daddy had been fortunate. Part of their good fortune came from living in a house that was so open that the pressure could not build up within its walls. But more than that, The Tornado had "passed over" instead of "touching down."

As soon as Mama and Daddy had finished their chores, they drove to Tulia to call us. The stories of The Tornado abounded. Some were true, and some were growing rumors. Daddy offhandedly remarked, "I felt like The Tornado picked up the house and turned it around three times before it put it back on the foundation." In an hour, he heard his "felt-like" story told as truth.

It had "weathered" a lot more than Mama and Daddy anticipated when we moved to the Rock Creek area. We had casually boarded the weather merry-go-round, expecting wind, snow, sand . . . wind, snow . . . wind . . . But the merry-go-round was actually a runaway roller coaster, carrying us on a wild ride through The Cold, The Blizzard, and The Tornado. When we finally came to a halt, we dizzily stepped off, knowing that we had been on an unforgettable ride. It was not a ride we wanted to repeat.

Wanda Gene's house in the Blizzard of 1940

Wanda Gene's father digging out the
windmill after the Blizzard of 1940

HANDMEDOWNISM AND SECONDHANDISM

No one would have chosen to wear the fashion labels, "Hand-Me-Down," "Homemade," and "Second Hand," but it was the Great Depression. By the end of the 1930s, "handmedownism" and "secondhandism" were worn-out concepts belonging to a worn-out people who handed down "hand-me-downs" and purchased third hand "second hands."

It seemed to be a propitious time to enter a new decade, the decade of the 1940s. There were indications that America was "comin' out" of the Depression and that "Store Bought" could become a way of life not known since the 1920s. Until the hope for the 1940s became a reality, however, a girl would wear a once bright purple, now faded blue dress, a boy would pin his too-large trousers with a safety pin, and a mother would cut cardboard from the Post Toasties box to cover the holes in her family's shoes. The farm families needed, desperately needed, a respite from their day-in, day-out drudgery. There was a dearth of entertainment—no TV, few radios, and not enough money to go to "picture shows." Thus, the Country School Program, existing long before the Depression Era, became a significant institution in the 1930s.

The Country School Program, a social event attended by the entire community, was a performance of hand-me-down "parts," "readin's," and skits, presented by kids in their best hand-me-down Sunday clothing, at the entertainment center of the community, the school. Most schools had a permanent stage of some description. The wealthier schools were the proud owners of splendid stage curtains, with elaborately embellished, multi-colored advertisements decorating every available inch of the heavy paper/oil cloth fabric. It was an honor to be chosen to pull the cord that raised and lowered the "winder shade" curtain. Only the strongest boys were given such a responsibility. If one lost control of the curtain cord, the curtain dropped, hitting the stage with a resounding thud. The community waited in hungry anticipation for the boy to raise the curtain.

Before I was three, several years before we moved to the Rock Creek area, "someone" had begun volunteering me as a "filler" at school programs. I was an "old hand" at walking out on the stage, casting a quick glance upward to make sure I was not standing beneath the curtain, which might fall, and repeating inane lines:

> Christmas time is coming
> Lawsy, Lawsy me,
> Everyone is running 'round
> Happy as they can be.

Or worse:

> My Daddy says
> The only reason he
> Doesn't give me to
> Somebody for a sweet
> Christmas present
> Is 'cause he couldn't
> Get along without me
> I'se so nice.

"Lawsy" and "I'se" weren't even good West Texese grammar. The readin' I hated the most was one that I performed twice before I was six. My dislike came from being told to "act out the readin'" as I spoke the lines:

> I'm a very little creature,
> But I'm large enough to show
> How the ladies trip on Broadway
> When they want to catch a beau.
> This is just the way they wiggle,
> Up and down the streets they go
> Smiling sweetly every moment
> When they want to catch a beau.

I was not overjoyed when I heard that Rock Creek would have a Christmas Program. It was planned for 22 December to accommodate a number of families who did not choose to have a separate Christmas celebration at home. There was little travel during the Depression, certainly no vacation travel. No one was "comin' home" or "goin' home" for Christmas at Rock Creek in 1939. Everyone in the community would be able to attend.

When we entered Rock Creek School on the night of the program, I found myself in a strange building. There was one room instead of two, the partition having been folded back. Flickering kerosene lanterns, hanging from hooks that I had not previously noticed, softened the uglier features of the room. There was a stage—planks laid across railroad ties. Since there was no permanent curtain, a makeshift curtain had been made by hanging bed sheets over wire. The desks had been rearranged, allowing the extremely low stage to be viewed more readily. A sparsely decorated, scraggly tree stood in the corner. Even the kids, dressed in their hand-me-down Sunday best, were strangers. I stayed close to Mama, much as I had done four months earlier on the first day of school.

I was glad I did NOT have to give a readin' at the program. My only assignment was to join in singing "Santa Claus is Coming to Town" (all four verses), "Hang Up Your Stocking," and "The Merry Christmas Tree." We sang without instruments or tune. I doubt that anyone knew the tunes since few had benefit of radio or phonograph. The audience didn't care; they gave enthusiastic approval. We were merely the introduction. Santa was the program. As soon as we had sung the last word of the last verse, the door banged open and Santa entered with a bulky towsack of gifts thrown over his shoulder. There was a buzz of whispers:

"Et's Mr. Miller."

"No, I thank that et's Pete."

"Naw, Pete's sittin' over thar. Et must be Mr. Carter."

It didn't require much time to discover "who" was missing in the audience.

Since it was the custom for families at Rock Creek to exchange their family gifts at the community Christmas tree, Mama warned me several times, "You probably won't receive but one gift, the gift from the one who drew your name. You know that we'll give our gifts at Granny's house on Christmas Day." I knew who had drawn my name, knew who was obligated to buy me a present. It was Betty Ann, the girl whom I had popped with my handkerchief. I found myself casting meaningful glances at her . . . wondering . . . Betty Ann gave me a blank stare in return. I knew that Mama was beginning to doubt that I would receive a gift because she kept repeating, "Now don't say anything. It'll be all right if you don't get a gift tonight. You'll get your gifts on Christmas Day."

It was embarrassing to watch everyone receive gifts while I sat and waited. The evening dragged miserably on, and Santa didn't once glance in my direction. There were only two gifts left under the tree when Santa called my name. I opened my present, looking at its contents without outward emotion, hearing Mama suggest, "I'm sure you will want to thank Betty Ann before we go home." Walking toward Betty Ann, I thought about the "part" I was about to recite: "Thank you very much for the handkerchief. I'm sure that I'll find a good use for it." Widening my mouth into a mock smile, I merely verbalized, "Thank you."

Valentine's Day would be an austere celebration, without refreshments or guests. We would give valentines, and, of course, we would have a program. Evidently, Mrs. Biggs had selected my readin' from its title, "February," without bothering to study the content. Rock Creek did not acknowledge Abraham Lincoln or celebrate his birthday. Yet, I stood before the class and recited without much ardor:

> There is a month of holidays
> That we like very well.
> It is the month of February
> About which we tell.
> Two birthdays then we celebrate—
> For Washington we cheer
> And Lincoln, the great President
> Whom we hold very dear.

I fervently hoped the bus would arrive before we had time to distribute the valentines. We had drawn names, but Mama had made a valentine for very kid in school. Instead of signing my name, she pasted a picture of me beneath her carefully printed "F-r-o-m." Although I silently questioned the popularity of the idea, she was positive that everyone at Rock Creek wanted a picture of me "to keep." One boy, opening his valentine, handed it to me, saying, "Et must be fer you. Et has yore picture." I handed it back to him without trying to explain why he had my picture. I really didn't know "why." One of the blessings of The Blizzard that snowbound us two days later was that everyone forgot about Valentine's Day.

Although the Easter Egg Hunt/All Day Picnic was not presented as a program, it had a hand-me-down script that was carefully followed. The picnic was held on the Friday before Easter in nearby Tule Canyon, the canyon that bounded the Cap (Cap Rock) on the east. Daddy took off work to join in the festive event. The weather was in complete harmony with the plans for the day—no wind, sand, or rain. Not having previously seen the canyon, I was amazed to find its rim green and its walls red, in contrast to the brown of the schoolground. At first I thought that the colorful dots on the canyon rim were wildflowers. To my joy, I discovered the "wildflowers" were actually dyed hen eggs, "hidden" in open sight among the prickly pear, mesquites, and gyp (gypsum rock). With excitement and anticipation, I joined the other kids to prepare to hunt the eggs.

Before long we were alerted, "Get rea-----dee." Mr. Biggs began to walk up and down the "start" line, repeating in his stentorian voice, "The little kids not in school get to go first. The rest of you—wait." Disappointment rolled over me as I watched the mothers, with a little help from their small children, pick the prairie clean. Once again Mr. Biggs gave his instructions, "School kids start beyond that stump." Although I ran as fast as I could, the stampeding herd of older school kids soon outdistanced my second grade legs. The Easter Egg Hunt was over before it began for me. I didn't want anyone, NOT ANYONE to ask, "How minny's in yore sack?" I was ready to go home.

The men and older boys and girls started the traditional softball game, while the younger kids began their version of the Easter Parade in the rattlesnake-infested canyon. We had never played in segregated groups of boys and girls at school, and I was puzzled when we dawdled on the canyon rim until the boys began to wind their way down into the canyon. I was delighted when we met the boys and opened my mouth to greet them. Quickly, I was cautioned, "Shhh. We don't speak to boys in the canyon." I was dumbfounded. We didn't speak to the boys we played with at school every day? Turning their heads the girls admired the red canyon walls, ignoring the boys who were walking within ten feet of us. Surely, having been snowbound together merited a nod of acknowledgment. But not a word was uttered by the boys or the girls. As we were returning from our walk, we met the boys again, repeating the same scenario. I have often wondered what would have happened had I yelled, "Let's 'Pop the Whip'."

At last the girls grew tired of meeting and ignoring the boys. As we slowly climbed out of the canyon, we saw an idyllic scene. The new mothers, sitting amidst the other women and children, were unashamedly nursing their babies. Some of the toddlers were investigating the bugs in the canyon grass. The men, having rolled their own cigarettes, were enjoying their "smokes" as much as they were enjoying the "good," "clean" jokes and riddles they were sharing:

Q. If the King of England is the Admiral of the Navy, what is the Duke of Windsor?

A. The third mate of an American destroyer!

Q. If Mrs. Lindberg, Mrs. Mussolini, the Duchess of Windsor, and Mrs. Roosevelt were playing cards, and Mrs. Lindberg drew an Ace, Mrs. Mussolini drew a Deuce, and the Duchess of Windsor drew a King, what would Mrs. Roosevelt do?

A. Ask for a New Deal.

Before long, the tenor of the jokes changed:

Q. Does a man have more sense after he gets married?

A. Yes, but it's too late!

Q. What is a woman?

A. A thing of beauty and a "jaw" forever!

Q. What's the difference between a woman and a bird-dog?

A. A bird-dog is a pointer and a setter, while a woman is a disappointer and an upsetter.

Q. What is an old maid?

A. Someone who has all the answers but has never been asked the question.

The hours began to drag. I had gone to the Easter Egg Hunt/Picnic with casual interest, only to be confronted by hand-me-down customs that left me miserable and puzzled. The day had been full of bewildering contradictions. The girls and boys played with each other at Rock Creek, but they ignored each other at Tule Canyon. The women thought it was wrong to speak of breasts in public, but they thought it was right to nurse a baby in front of anyone and everyone. The men at the picnic enjoyed the jokes about women, but Daddy held Granny and Mama in high esteem, loving, honoring and respecting them. My head was spinning with all of my unsolved riddles, and I longed to go home. I considered it a good sign when the men began to cast glances at the sun to determine the time of day. It would not be long before everyone had to leave to do the nightly chores.

By the end of the picnic, the "wildflower" eggs had been replaced by the day's trash and garbage, dotting the green landscape like small monuments to a rare outing. The families started home to perform their mundane chores, knowing it would be another year before they would attend such a magnificent picnic. I left, hoping I would never again be a part of an Easter Egg Hunt at Tule Canyon.

Handmedownism and secondhandism spread their tentacles from clothing to prejudices, ideas, and values, also worn without criticism in security and comfort. Oblivious to what was happening, we were all exposed to the deadly "Hand-Me-Down Syndrome." Only time would determine who would survive. No place offered a better breeding ground for the germs than the Country School Program.

A few weeks after the picnic, Mrs. Biggs produced some one-of-a-kind, well-worn skit books in preparation for the End of School Program to be held "'bout dark" on 10 May 1940. She handed me two books, one of skits and one of readings, told me my assignment for the program, and left no doubt about my responsibility: "Have your mother copy your part in the skit and your reading TONIGHT. We have to send these books home with a different kid every night. Remember! Bring the book back tomorrow with your parts copied." Looking at the books, I didn't know if I could keep them in one piece until they were safely returned to Mrs. Biggs. Mama copied my role in the skit and my reading, using a tablet and pencil. I watched her pause occasionally, musing aloud about the dress I would wear at this grand event.

I had a role in one of the choice hand-me-down skits at Rock Creek, a skit that always received great laughter and enthusiastic applause. It was called, "The 'Nigger' Doll Skit." It was a skit about a Beauty Contest for the dolls of white girls. Through some error, a "nigger" girl entered her "nigger" doll in the contest. Since Zonelle was the only girl who owned a "nigger" doll, she had the lead in the skit. I was not envious. On the night of the program, Zonelle would wear long black gloves, black stockings, her worst dress, an apron, a bandana, and have her face blackened with stove soot. Instead of using good Rural West Texese, she would talk like "one of them." Three or four of us would stand on the stage with our beautiful white dolls, pointing out their merits to the judge. In a quandary, the judge would decide in favor of Zonelle and her "nigger"

doll. As we marched off the stage in huffy indignation, we
would dump our dolls in a buggy.

I had two problems and a question from the outset.
I was to be the first one to dump my doll in the buggy.
Mama told me to wait until the last, carefully placing,
not dumping, Joy, my doll, on top of the other dolls in
the buggy. Knowing that school would be out and that I
would not have to face Mrs. Biggs again, I felt that I could
handle that problem. All I had to do was please Mrs. Biggs
when we were practicing without props and please Mama
on the night of the program. The second problem did not
have a solution. Every day Mrs. Biggs told us that we must
bring our dolls to school on the morning of the program,
leaving them at school until that night. Every day Mama
told me that I could not take Joy to school before the
night of the program. Mama prevailed. Mrs. Biggs was
not pleased when I arrived at school without my doll.
When the girls looked at me knowingly, I felt dreadfully
chagrined. I knew the girls thought my doll too good to
be taken to school. And the question? I phrased it as best
I could: "Why is this skit supposed to be funny?" When
I broke The Code by asking the other girls, they sighed
and rolled their eyes. When I broke The Code again and
asked Mama, she said, "Well, you know." I didn't know
in 1940, and I still don't know.

The night of the program finally arrived. The portable
stage with the sheets used for a curtain appeared again.
The production of the skit went as planned. "Everthang"
and "everbody" were forgiven in the aura of success.
The audience laughed uproariously and applauded

enthusiastically, not minding that older brothers and sisters had presented the identical program and worn the same clothes in prior years. With the skit behind me, I gave my readin' with enthusiasm:

> The grammars and the spellers,
> The pencils and the shears,
> The books that hold the fractions,
> And the books that tell the years,
> The crayons and the blackboards,
> And the map upon the wall,
> Must all be glad together
> They'll not be used 'til fall.

The End of School Program was over. All that remained on the night's agenda was the graduation of three or four eighth grade students. It was a "lived happily ever after" time for Rock Creek community. This was the "Decade of Hope," and these were the first graduates at Rock Creek in the 1940s. The community was justifiably proud of its graduates. Wistful comments were rampant:

"Their prospects are shore as shootin' bettern ours wuz."

"I've knowed everyone of them since they were borned."

"She's the first un in our bunch to git thet much larnin'."

It was a graduation without ceremony, pomp, or fanfare. The graduates walked to the stage in their "polish-over-scratches" brogans, their "let-down-hem" dresses, and their "too-short-sleeves" coats. Mr. Biggs was waiting for them on the stage. I thought, but I was not sure, that he gave a fleeting smile as he told them in plain, simple language that they would enter high school in the fall.

It was not the time for a Depression Era school to add frills to its graduation program. And Rock Creek didn't. There was no invocation. There were no graduation speeches with the customary challenges and histrionics. The graduates had already met a lifetime of challenges in handmedownism and secondhandism. There were no diplomas, just report cards. There was no benediction. The graduation ceremony "ended when it was over"—no delay, no "wrappin' up," no farewell.

Mama, Daddy, Granny, and I started walking across the hard dirt schoolground toward the car. And, if we had thoughts, we did not share them. Daddy took time to light his pipe. Mama proudly and lovingly carried Joy, patting her hair and straightening her dress. Granny, as always, held my hand, occasionally giving it a gentle squeeze. I did not look back. Although I did not know it, my education at Rock Creek was over. Never again was I in Rock Creek School after the night of 10 May 1940. Never again did I see Mr. and Mrs. Biggs. Never again did I see twenty-two of the twenty-six students.

No simile, metaphor, hyperbole, or euphemism could describe my year at Rock Creek better than the Rural West Texese words of Hanner, one of the graduates: "We dun dun et, hain't we?"

The Easter egg hunt at Tule Canyon

Wanda Gene and her doll Joy

Notes

AN IDYLLIC REALISM

1. Jeff Davis Pie is a five generation family recipe, first used by my great grandmother, Mattie Creamer Morgan. Granny began making the pies when she married in 1907. Mama took over the task. I think the pie was named for the President of the Confederacy.

    2 cups sugar
    4 tablespoons flour
    1 teaspoon cinnamon
    1 teaspoon allspice
    ½ teaspoon nutmeg
    ½ cup butter
    4 eggs—beaten
    1 ½ cup sweet milk
    1 teaspoon vanilla

Cook in raw crust—2 pies
Since the pie dates back to the days of cooking in a coal stove, no degrees or baking time were given.

"IT WAS TIME TO START TO SCHOOL"

1. "Found" meant "gave birth to." Births—kittens, puppies, calves, lambs, ponies—were regular events on farms. Farmers used the polite word "found" to describe the birth, thus removing sex from the event.
2. The teacherage was a house on the schoolground, provided by the school district, for the use of teachers.
3. An official description of Rock Creek School is given by the Briscoe County Historical Society: "Once named Coker, School District Number Four is better known as Rock Creek. The first school held there was in January 1892, with a four-month term . . . The Rock Creek School was located in a pasture on the J. A. Ranch seven miles west of Silverton."
4. Philadelphia Red Cake is a Harris recipe.

1 ½ cup sugar
2/3 cup butter
3 eggs
½ cup sour milk
1/3 teaspoon salt

6 tablespoons cocoa
½ teaspoon soda
1 ½ cup flour
1 teaspoon vanilla

Dissolve cocoa in warm water. Add soda
and let cool. Mix sugar and butter. Add
egg yolks. Add sour milk and salt. Add
cocoa and flour at same time. Add beaten
egg whites. Add vanilla.

To make sour milk, add vinegar to sweet
milk. Since the pie dates back to the days
of cooking in a coal stove, no degrees or
baking time were given.

"WAIT 'TIL AFTER COTTON PICKIN'"

1. Daddy had an opportunity to study penmanship
under the lady who later illustrated Penmanship
books. She encouraged Daddy to find elaborate
capital letters on billboards. When he saw
a letter that he liked, he spent hours copying,
perfecting, and incorporating the letter into his
own handwriting. People always remarked about
his beautiful penmanship.

2. AAA was the Agricultural Adjustment
Administration, inaugurated in the beginning of
government aid and control of farms. Daddy went
from farm to farm, measuring land, determining

how many acres were planted, drawing maps of the farms, and then writing reports.

3. Radiator caps were like gasoline caps. The radiator was at the front of the car, beneath the hood. The opening of the radiator was on top of the hood and covered with a cap at the location where car emblems now appear. The driver had to unscrew the radiator cap frequently to fill the radiator with water.

WHEN AUTHORITY BECAME TYRANNY

1. In Red Rover, there were two teams, about thirty to fifty feet apart. One team called, "Red Rover, Red Rover, let Wanda Gene come over." I was called because I was a little girl. I ran toward the other line, seeking to break the line at its weakest point, usually between two girls. If I broke the grip, I took two prisoners home. If not, I became a member of the other team.

2. In Three Deep, the players were divided into pairs and the pairs were in a circle. A member of each pair was standing behind the other. There were two remaining players; one was "It" and one was "Catcher." The Catcher chased It until It stopped behind one of the pairs. This made it Three Deep instead of Two Deep. The person in front of the Three Deep group became It and had to escape the Catcher. The only way the Catcher could

become It was to catch someone when they were running.

3. In Wolf Over the River, two sides lined up forty to fifty feet apart. The "Wolf" was in the middle (of the river) between the lines. The Wolf yelled, "Wolf Over the River." The lines ran towards the other side. The Wolf tried to tag as many persons as possible before they crossed the safety line.

4. The boys were allowed to practice at playing marbles. This was known as "funsies." They could not play "keepsies," a gambling game with the winner getting to keep the other boys' marbles.

5. Mumblepeg was played with an ordinary jackknife that had a ½ inch wide blade about 2 ½ inches long in one end and a smaller blade in the other end. Only the long blade was used in the game. The objective was to complete the most intricate maneuvers without failing to stick the blade in the ground. The maneuvers were in order with each maneuver being done right-handed and then left-handed.

6. Winkum was a social game. Boys stood behind the chairs of girls. One chair was vacant. The boy behind the vacant chair "winked" at one of the girls. The object was for the girl to run across to the empty chair before the boy behind her chair put his arms around her and grabbed her. If the girl preferred the boy standing behind her, she did not try very hard to get away.

7. Spin the Bottle was also a social game. Boys and girls alternated sitting in a circle. A boy would spin the bottle. If it pointed at one of the opposite sex, he would kiss her. If it pointed to one of the same sex, he would spin again.

THE CODE OF THE THREE MONKEYS

1. According to the whispers I overheard, Daddy's brother Cliff had a drinking problem and occasionally spent time in jail. He was also an accomplished luthier, making around 150 violins in his lifetime, the first when he was 24 years old. On 22 August 1945, the <u>Amarillo Globe News</u> reported: "In Los Angeles, St. Louis, and New York City, the violin made by Cliff Harris of Amarillo was proclaimed the finest piece of workmanship in the United States. Its tone is absolutely perfect and Harris has been offered fabulous prices by several of the top-ranking musicians of our time. It has been appraised by experts at $2,300. However, the violin is not for sale at any price, and Harris declares that as soon as materials become available, he intends to put his patent before the world." Four months later Cliff was dead at the age of 49, and the violin was found in the possession of another man. The man said that Cliff owed him $100 and had given him the violin until he could pay him. Daddy

suspected murder but received no cooperation from the Amarillo police.

"IT WEATHERED A LOT"

1. Black Draught was a medicine for catarrh. In conjunction with Black Draught, drug stores produced calendars.

HANDMEDOWNISM AND SECONDHANDISM

1. Betty Ann's mother probably did not know about the incident with the wet handkerchief. Certainly, Mama didn't. The general method of purchasing gifts for someone whose name was drawn was for the parent to buy the gift without consulting the giver.

2. According to <u>The Handbook of Texas</u>, "Tule Canyon merges with Palo Duro Canyon in western Briscoe County. Tule Canyon, noted for the beauty of its colorful walls and for the unusual formations created by centuries of erosion, has been identified as one of the canyons encountered by Francisco Vasquez de Coronado in 1542 and as one crossed by the Texas Santa Fe Expedition in 1841. The last major Indian engagement in Texas was fought in Tule and Palo Duro Canyons in September, 1874, when R. S. Mackenzie defeated the Comanche."

3. The Handbook of Texas also describes the Cap Rock: ". . . a highly mineral layer which underlies the Llano Estacado, is so called because it caps the area and thus protects the sediments beneath it from erosion . . . Although the term Cap Rock technically applies only to the formation itself, the expression is often loosely used to mean the whole Llano Estacado area."

4. Walter Bean, his two brothers, and I rode a bus together during the following two years, going to the town school of Kress. Of all the kids who attended Rock Creek in 1939, Walter became the most prominent, serving on boards and committees in Briscoe County.

Printed in the United States
By Bookmasters